THE FISHING SMART
ANYWHERE
HANDBOOK FOR SALT WATER &
FRESH WATER

Bob Banfelder

BB

~~

BROADWATER BOOKS

Riverhead, New York

Broadwater Books
141 Riverside Drive
Riverhead, New York 11901

The Library of Congress Cataloging-in-Publication Data is available on file.

ISBN 978-0-9859486-1-0

Printed in the United States of America

10 9 8 7 6 5 4 3 2 1

Bob Banfelder

The Fishing Smart *Anywhere* Handbook for Salt Water & Fresh Water

Bob Banfelder is an award-winning novelist and outdoors writer. His articles have appeared in numerous outdoors publications; e.g., *Nor'east Saltwater, The Fisherman, On The Water, Big Game Fishing Journal, Hana Hou! The Magazine for Hawaiian Airlines, New York Game & Fish*. Banfelder presently maintains a monthly online report for *Nor'east Saltwater*. He is a member of the Long Island Outdoor Communicators Network and the New York State Outdoor Writer's Association.

Bob also co-hosts (with Donna Derasmo) Cablevision TV's *Special Interests with Bob & Donna*. They have interviewed a number of outdoors enthusiasts, artists and writers such as Bob Bourguignon, Eileen Gerle, Pat Mundus, Christopher Paparo, and Tony Salerno.

In addition to his writing for the great outdoors, Bob has written five psychological thrillers: *No Stranger Than I, The Author, The Teacher, Knots* and *Trace Evidence. The Author and The Teacher*, the first and second books in the Justin Barnes series, both received "Best Suspense Book" accolades from NewBookReviews. *Knots* is the third thriller in the Justin Barnes series. *The Good Samaritans*, the final in the series, is scheduled for publication in 2014. Banfelder weaves his knowledge and love of the outdoors through his novels.

www.RobertBanfelder.com
Facebook @Robert Banfelder
Twitter @RBanfelder.

Acknowledgments

Acknowledgments for a work that covers the span of sixty years can be a daunting endeavor, for I must delve deep into my memory bank to recall all those fabulous folks who have helped Donna and me course a watery path in order to bring this guidebook to the surface. There are those authors whom I have read but never met yet have had a tremendous influence upon my psyche. Conversely, there are those whom I have met at talks, seminars, fishing clubs and related organizations. Too, there are those souls with whom Donna and I have fished, clammed and crabbed followed up by sitting down and sharing our seafood catch. Additionally, there are others whom I have instructed, the great irony being that you almost always learn from those you teach.

Also, there are publishers, editors, artists, photographers, columnists, marketing people and boating captains to thank here as well. Their names, in addition to those alluded to above, would fill a tome. What to do? Well, in order for the acknowledgments not to surpass the length of the book itself, I decided to thank all those, both past and present, who have had the most impact on the course of Donna's and my successes.

Finally, there is the fear of forgetting to name a special someone, that person knowing full well that he or she, too, had contributed in helping this fishing fool and his companion see this work come to full fruition. Therefore, if you fail to see your name listed below, take solace in realizing that my apology is sincere.

Sal Amendolia, Ron Atkinson, Don Avendolia, Chris Babcock, Captain Len Belcaro, Kevin Blinkoff, Gene Bourque, Neil Buchler, Captain Dan Buckley, Jr., Captain Ken Birmingham, Brendan P. Byrne, Bob Clouser, Thomas Cousins, Joe Cravotta, Captain John DeMaio, Dan Eng, Jimmy Fee, Gene and Susan Frohnhoefer, Tom Gahan, Eileen Carpino-Gerle, Paul Gianelli, Fred Golofaro, Ed Goodfield, Emiel Grinsberg, Harvey Holmes, Captain Ken Holmes, Captain Nick Karas, "Crazy" Alberto Knie, Bernard "Lefty" Kreh, Bob Lindquist, John Mazurkiewicz, Enzo Magnozzi, Tom Melton, Jack Meyer, Captain Pete Mikoleski, Captain Tom Mikoleski, Bruce Morabito, Captain Frank Mundus, Wayne Nester, Carlee Ogeka, Captain Christopher and Candyce Paparo, Angelo Peluso, Bob Popovics, Nicholas Posa, Artie Prevete, Captain Mike Russo, Tony Salerno, Ed Scalice, George Scocca, Don Schaefer, Tom Schlichter, Carl Schnitter, Michael Shapiro, Richard Siberry, John Skinner, Richard "Doc" Steinberger, Lou Tabory, Jim Teeny, William A. 'Doc' Muller, Bob Veverka, Tom Wernikowski

Special mention goes out to Jason Banfelder, Professor Emeritus Robert Dore, Betty and Edward Fitch, Geoffrey Freeman, Nancy and Richard Roberts, Dr. Luce Skrabanek, JoAnn Zenewitz. You folks unquestionably assisted in getting this book project off the ground by subscribing to my *Fishing Salt & Fresh Water ~ Hunting ~ Eating Well* guide. You have my sincerest gratitude.

Bob Banfelder
April 2013

Contents

THE FISHING SMART *ANYWHERE* HANDBOOK FOR SALT WATER & FRESH WATER

Bob Banfelder

Introduction

Welcome to the premiere edition of "The Fishing Smart *Anywhere* Handbook for Salt Water & Fresh Water."

As an award-winning author, I embrace (along with my companion of over forty years, Donna) a number of water-related activities. Sixty years of experience went into writing this concise yet comprehensive guide. If I had to sum up this handbook in a single word, it is all about having **Fun**. Be it spin casting, bait casting or the supposed arcane art of fly casting, together we will target new tackle, examine time-tested techniques, and apply innovative approaches to these three basic methods —methods that will give the angler the added edge.

Whether saltwater or freshwater fishing, clamming, crabbing, kayaking, cooking seafood or smoking fish, selecting the proper equipment is of paramount importance. The information presented will prove priceless, providing you with practical advice, serious savings, unprecedented quality and value. That's a promise, not hyperbole. Get it right the first time, and avoid unnecessary aggravation and expense.

Taking fresh fish and shellfish from our seas and shores is rewarding, for there is a world of delectable fare that awaits you. Perfected over the course of many years, I present gourmet recipes that will delight you, your family and friends.

Written in an informative, entertaining and often humorous fashion, this handbook is for the beginner, intermediate as well as the advanced outdoors enthusiast, serving as either a condensed treatment of a subject or a concise reference. I offer you a unique approach in that this information is superbly blended and balanced to accommodate *all* levels of experience—from introducing and instructing newcomers to many enjoyable and rewarding water-related activities, to presenting veteran outdoorsmen/women with creative techniques.

Residing on the water, Donna and I live, sleep, breathe and share our outdoor experiences with you. Having spent sixty years plying the waters along the eastern seaboard, we have made the East End of Long Island our home and playground for the past twenty-three years. We have been praised by Angelo Peluso—outdoors author, columnist and avid fisherman—as the "Best writing and fishing tag-team on Long Island." I invite you to join Donna and me on our continual journey.

Living the good life is yours for the taking.

Chapter 1

*SELECTING HIGH QUALITY <u>ULTRA-LIGHT TO MEDIUM-ACTION</u>
SALTWATER & FRESHWATER <u>SPINNING REELS</u>
& MATCHING RODS*

<u>Miniature</u> Weapons of Mass Destruction

A Lightweight but Gutsy Arsenal for the Suds and Sweetwater

Top to bottom: Stradic 1000 MgFB; Sustain 1000 FE; Stella 3000 FD; Sustain 3000 FE

There are an overwhelming number of rods and reels on the market today, many manufacturers and models from which to choose. The problem of selection can be overwhelming. How does one begin to sift through a mountain of information in order to make an intelligent decision? A good deal of research and extensive field-testing were conducted before arriving at a definitive conclusion. Not only were these rods and reels field-tested, Donna, my significant other, and I own over a dozen models. Therefore, you can count on the fact that these products have been thoroughly *handled*.

In helping to put a quality spinning rod and reel in your hands that will last untold years, if not a lifetime, we are going to start by narrowing the playing field, plying our inshore waters as opposed to, say, hunting sharks in a deep blue sea. For the latter, you would generally want a conventional baitcasting outfit, not that you couldn't tackle the pelagic division on a spinning outfit. Frank Mundus (world famous shark fisherman) had served a good many customers who, over the course of several decades, did exactly that. Many anglers like Mark Sedotti and Angelo Peluso hunt for and have tackled sharks with a fly rod. But for openers we'll stay close to home, fishing our coastal waters, bays, estuaries, rivers, lakes and ponds. Proceeding in the following fashion will save you considerable time and money.

First off, let's select a highly respected and reputable spinning reel manufacturer. There are three companies that I highly recommend within a competitive price range—Shimano, Daiwa, and Penn—and in that order. Let's stick with my first pick: Shimano. I suggest downloading their online catalog, covering both spinning and conventional reels and rods. Their current catalog can still be overwhelming. However, with this book in hand, you have just eliminated tons of research and are in a superior arena. Together, we will explore Shimano's ultra-light, light, medium, and medium/heavy spinning reels, marrying them to quality rods, and not necessarily Shimano's. We'll home in on several superb lightweight spinning reels for saltwater applications, which will certainly do double duty in freshwater situations. Too, we'll examine a few featherweights for freshwater fanatics. While perusing Shimano's line of spinning reels, you will note several series, such as **Stella, Sustain and Stradic**, to mention but only a few of many models. I've just named those three with which you should concern yourself for reasons I'll cover momentarily. Within each series, Shimano's catalog will note different model numbers, specifying size among other important considerations; that is, line retrieve per crank measured in inches, line capacity measured in pound test/plus yardage, maximum drag setting—measured in pounds, number of ball bearings and roller bearings, gear ratio, grip shape, weight of the reel measured in ounces, and price (MSRP).

Do not concern yourself with that last entry just yet. I know—easy for me to say; perhaps hard for you to do initially. One of the important elements you should consider in selecting any reel is the number of ball bearings it contains. This will help determine a reel's smoothness.

In this and the next two chapters, you will note letter designations following particular models as they relate to Shimano's Stella, Sustain and Stradic spinning reels. For example, Stella FD has recently been changed to FE, Sustain FE to FG, Stradic FI to FG, et cetera. These letters reflect modifications or refinements in design that have been made for the current year; that is, 2013. Some reels have been updated while others have remained exactly the same for the past several years. I'll cover these recent improvements as we proceed. The important thing to keep in mind is that a Stella spinning reel is of superior craftsmanship, followed by Sustain and Stradic.

The new Stella FE series has 14 ball bearings plus one roller bearing; four models from which to choose. The new Sustain FG has 7 ball bearings and one roller bearing; seven models to seriously consider. The new Stradic CI^4 1000 F as well as the Stradic CI^4 1000 MFL have 6 ball bearings and one roller bearing.

Some series such as Shimano's Baitrunner has 3 ball bearings. Others have one or zero ball bearings and no roller bearings. Why do manufacturers do this? Answer: to reach a wider market; to *reel* you in. Don't waste your money with these less expensive reels or you'll be labeled, and rightfully so, penny-wise and pound-foolish.

Here is how I carefully went about selecting two of Shimano's superior medium-action spinning reels that Donna and I use for either saltwater or freshwater applications. Next, two of Shimano's light-action reels that we reserve strictly for freshwater applications. The quartet will cover virtually any situation ranging from ultra-light to medium action.

Of great importance, too, is the reel's drag system. Next, seriously consider the weight of the reel. A light but gutsy reel, both literally and figuratively speaking, will have you casting effortlessly. A heavy reel will tire you out quickly. The high-caliber Shimano spinning reels referencing Stella, Sustain and Stradic are, indeed, gutsy reels. Upon noting the size of say a Stella 3000 FD or FE, you might not, at first, believe so. That's understandable. They are small (approximately 4¼ inches; 6 inches in overall length with their handles extended rearward). They are light (8.2/8.1 ounces, respectively). Yet, I have seen the Stella 3000 FD tackle and bring a 70-pound billfish to boat. That's pretty gutsy!

Comparing the weight of a Stella 3000 FE, 8.1 ounces to that of the lightest Shimano Baitrunner B series, 19.8 ounces, you've now got the picture in terms of those extremes. Of course, Shimano has a legion of models from which to choose. Some are even heavier, some lighter. After considering the number of bearings, drag system and reel weight for inshore waters, I elected to go with the Stella 3000 FD as one of our four choices for the suds. I was not disappointed. You'll simply consider the newer Stella FE series.

I opted for the next two reels from the Sustain FE series. The lightest of the lot, the Sustain 1000 FE, weighs only 7.4 ounces; it carries 7 ball bearings and one roller bearing. Donna will use it for light freshwater fishing, loading one of the extra spools with 110 yards of 6-pound test monofilament line, the other with braided line. The reel is capable of exerting a maximum drag setting of 7 pounds. The Sustain 3000 FE at 9.5 ounces, boasting the same number of bearings but sporting a Salt Water T-Type grip, is my inshore reel. Loading one of two spools with 140 yards of 10-pound test monofilament, the reel's maximum drag setting of 15 pounds, will certainly put the brakes on a good-sized striped bass or blue. Keep in mind that given their pound-test equivalents, braid will offer greater line capacity than mono. We'll cover monofilament, fluorocarbon and braided lines in other chapters.

Donna's light, little freshwater friend is from the Stradic 1000 MgFB series, weighing in at 7 ounces. With a magnesium frame and sideplate, this seemingly innocuous tool spooled with 110 yards of 6-pound test mono line, maximum drag setting of 7 pounds, will easily slow down a wiry pickerel along its watery path.

However, the reel has been discontinued, supplanted by Shimano's new CI^4 construction, a reinforced carbon fiber material that costs less to produce yet is stronger than steel and lighter than magnesium. The savings on the new Stradic CI^4 1000 F as well as the Stradic CI^4 1000 FML (designed for Microline), weighing in at 6 ounces and 6.1 ounces, respectively, is passed on to the consumer. MSRP for either reel is $199.99. That's $20 less than Donna's coveted Stradic 1000 MgFB, which translates into a definite bargain for the ultimate in ultra-lightweight spinning reels. No, I'm not going to run out and buy Donna a new one. She'll just have to live with that extra ounce.

All told, the Sustain and Stradic model series are superb spinning reels, eclipsed solely by their flagship Stella FE and Stella SW series.

You'll lay out $730 to $950 (MSRP) for Shimano's top-of-the-line Stella SW, **S**alt **W**ater, series. I selected, instead, for openers, one of their four Stella FD models ranging between $600 and $700. Here is where some confusion may lie. Does the FD or FE series mean that it is not designated for saltwater applications, whereas the SW series most definitely is? No, not really. Then what *is* the difference? Why the ambiguous "not really" qualifier? Good questions and important ones. The answer is that the Stella SW series does *not* have an anti-reverse switch as does the Stella FD or the current FE models. The SW series is engaged in a permanent anti-reverse mode, which means that the handle cannot be turned rearward. This prevents saltwater intrusion. Only if I'd be surfcasting in the suds in chest waders from the shore, jetty or such, where the wind and saltwater spray could play havoc upon the reel—which is not my intent with the Stella 3000 FD, as it is used from a boat in our bays—would I then elect to go with a member of the Stella SW series. I'd consider the Stella 5000 SW, the lightest in its lineup. You might ask, "Well, why didn't you just pay the difference (in this case, another $80) and be done with it as the Stella 5000 SW could perform double-duty, covering both inshore and offshore applications?" The answer is that I'd be moving into a heavier reel weighing 14.3 ounces as opposed to 8.2 ounces, not to mention wielding a heavier rod and more than likely heavier pound test line and lure. Casting for hours can take its toll. Donna and I feel that lighter outfits, especially worked from a boat on our bays, are the way to go. Besides, we enjoy the fight more with light but worthy tackle. In Chapter 2, we'll cover heavier-action reels.

Perusing the number of reel series Shimano presents may still prove confusing as to what is and what is not saltwater *approved*. Apart from the anti-reverse switch, if you properly maintain your equipment (both reel and rod) upon returning from a fishing trip, you can use many of their reels in the suds, for most have waterproof drag systems, anti-rust bearings, and protective coatings. The choices that the company offers are considerable. Again, preview their online catalog, which will also serve as an excellent reference.

For 2013, while contemplating ultra-light to medium-action spinning reels, consider the new Stradic CI^4 1000 FML along with the CI^4 1000 F ($199.99 each); Sustain 1000 FG ($329.99); Sustain 3000 FG ($329.99); Stella 3000 FE ($729.99). Keep in mind that you often get what you pay for. A $20 or $60 reel is not going to perform nor last like a $200 or $700 reel. That is the fact of the matter. You'll thank me in both the short and long run. Still can't justify spending the kind of monies mentioned? Here's something running along the lines of a rationalization, but one that just may convince you otherwise. It rests in your selection of a spinning rod to match one of Shimano's finer reels.

Matching Spinning Rods to Reels

Time and again, I see folks paying way too much money for fishing rods, whether it is a fly rod, baitcasting rod, or spinning rod. Quite frankly, you're wasting your money if you spend more than $30 to $40 on a spinning rod for the reels just covered. Shimano, Okuma and Ugly Stick (spelled Stik) rods are rated as the best spinning rods—but not in that order. However, they are priced in that order from the highest to the lowest cost: Shimano's Cumara–$210; Okuma's Guide Select–$90; Shakespeare's model SP 1100 Ugly Stik–$30 to $40. As you *generally* get what you pay for, folks automatically get talked into and/or simply reach for the more expensive rods. The fact is that the Ugly Stik is tougher than the other two rods that cost considerably more.

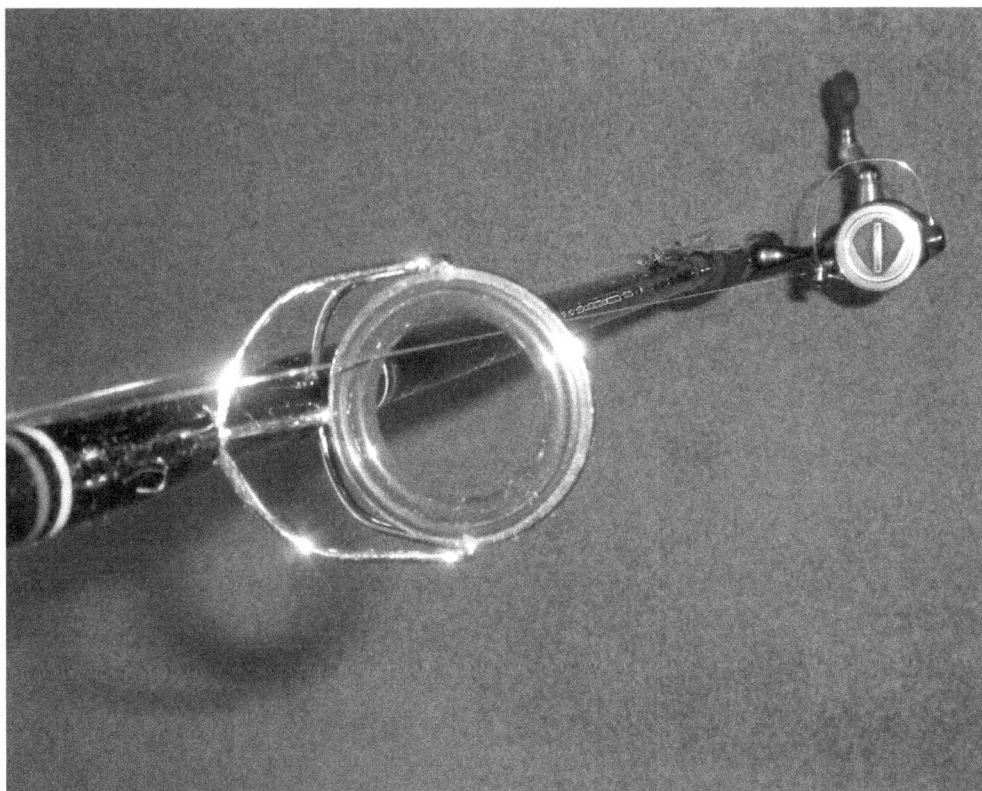

Ugly Stik Double-footed, Chrome-plated Stainless Steel Fuji Guides

You will gain a bit more sensitivity and wield slightly less weight with the Okuma Guide Select; however, the rod is simply not as strong as an Ugly Stik. The Shimano Cumara is a high-end wand that is also a tad more sensitive and lighter in weight. But it does not have the backbone of the two-piece SP 1100 7-foot medium-action (designed for 6-15 lb. test line) Ugly Stik. We're spooled with 10-pound test monofilament on my Stella FD 3000 model as well as Donna's Sustain FE 3000. I find the Ugly Stik SP 1100, 6½-foot equivalent too stiff, so I suggest the 7 footer. Different strokes for different folks. Too, these Fuji double-footed, chrome-plated stainless steel guides with aluminum oxide inserts and center bridges for extra ring support on the 1100 series simply can't be beat in terms of strength and durability. You will not likely find these superior guides on other rods that command significantly higher price tags. Perhaps you can now justify putting the money that I hopefully saved you toward a superior Stella, Sustain or Stradic reel. As I mentioned a moment ago, it may seem somewhat of a rationalization but a good one.

The Shimano Sustain 1000 FE and the Stradic 1000 MgFB models, coupled to matching Ugly Stik rods, are the outfits that Donna and I use for light down to ultra-light freshwater applications, respectively. You'll simply select the current Sustain 1000 FG and/or those Stradic 1000 CI[4] models.

For medium-action saltwater applications, you'll merely substitute our Stella 3000 FD and Sustain 3000 FE models with those respective FE and FG reels.

<u>Matching Medium-Action Shimano Spinning Reels with Shakespeare's Medium-Action Ugly Stik Rods for Saltwater Applications</u>

Shimano Sustain 3000 FG matched with Ugly Stik SP 1166-1M 6' 6"(1.98m) Action: Medium (6-15 lb. test line): one piece; cork grip
or
Ugly Stik SP 1100 7' 0" (2.10m) Action: Medium (6-15 lb. test line): two piece; foam grip

Shimano Stella 3000 FE matched with Ugly Stik SP 1100 7' 0" (2.10m) Action: Medium (6-15 lb. test line): two piece; foam grip

<u>Matching Light & Ultra-Lightweight Shimano Spinning Reels with Shakespeare's Light and Ultra-light Ugly Stik Rods for Freshwater Applications</u>

Shimano Sustain 1000 FG, or the Stradic CI[4] F matched with Shakespeare's two-piece Ugly Stik SPL 1102 6'6" (1.98m) Action: Light (4–10 lb. test line) 01B12CM

Shimano Stradic 1000 CI[4] FML matched with Shakespeare's two-piece Ugly Stik SPL 1102 5'0" (1.52m) Action: UL **Ultra-Light** (2–6 lb. test line) 01K11CM

These rod blanks feature the Howald-Built Process, consisting of graphite for strength and E-glass for flexibility. Blank-through-handle construction wedded to its signature Clear Tip design offers both strength and sensitivity from butt to apex. Super lightweight but durable EVA (Ethylene Vinyl Acetate) foam grips add a measure of comfort to every cast. Graphite twist-lock reel seats are standard on these two rods. Guides and tip are constructed from black stainless steel with aluminum oxide inserts. Consider these combos, and you're good to go.

Added to a lengthy list of features that make Shimano's top-of-the-line reels what they are (which I've elaborated on in Chapter 2), I'll address two new refinements here for 2013.

*You'll hear the term <u>X-Ship technology</u>, and you'll find it in both the Sustain FG series and the Stradic FJ series. What this results in is a super-smooth and powerful retrieve when fighting fish. Without getting too technical, the direct-drive gear and pinion gear have been redesigned and repositioned to mesh perfectly to give fluid performance.

*Shimano's Sustain FG series includes a <u>Rapid Fire Drag System</u>. Instead of having to turn the drag's dial two or three times in order to increase or decrease tension, turning the front dial's setting clockwise or counterclockwise but a fraction of what you normally would, quickly allows you to cover a full range of either maximum or minimum pressure. The Sustain 1000 FG 6½ ounce lightweight can apply the brakes to 7 pounds. That's some serious stopping power for a small but mighty reel.

Chapter 2

SELECTING HIGH QUALITY <u>MEDIUM/MEDIUM-HEAVY</u> ACTION SALTWATER & FRESHWATER <u>SPINNING</u> REELS & MATCHING RODS

<u>Major Weapons</u> of Mass Destruction

Why in the world would anyone spend between $730 and $950 for a spinning reel? This is Shimano's retail price range for their six Stella SW, **S**alt **W**ater, series. Well, it's a very good question and deserving of no less than a direct and honest answer—without any salesmanship rhetoric—just the facts. The Stella SW series delivers stellar performance. Succinctly stated, Stella SW models are outstanding. They are star performers.

What makes them so stellar?

Let's highlight this universe—star by star:

Stella SW Series 8000 SW & 5000 SW Saltwater Spinning Reels

*Stella's SW <u>waterproof drag system</u> is built upon superior technology. Their smaller sized 5000 SW exerts a maximum of 29 pounds of pressure. The five larger sizes—8000 SW, 8000 SWPG, 10000 SW, 18000 SW, and 20000 SW models—exercise a maximum drag of 55 pounds. That's some very serious stopping power.

The 5000 SW does this in a lightweight package of only 14.3 ounces. The 8000 SW middleweight champion applies the brakes while weighing in at 23.7 ounces. The heavyweight champ in the series is their 20000 SW, fashioned in a solid framework of 30.2 ounces. Needless to say, these superior drags are indeed waterproof, sealed with rubber gaskets to preclude saltwater intrusion.

*Maximizing strength and durability are what set Shimano's direct drive and pinion gears apart from the crowd. An amalgamation of metals (aluminum, brass, stainless steel), through time-tested technology, is the magic that led to the <u>Paladin Cold-Forging Process.</u> Die-cast components found in more affordable reels are prevalent because they are cheaper to manufacture, but they are neither strong nor as lasting as Shimano's cold-forging methods, which yield a smoother, lightweight product for prominent performance.

*Without getting *too* technical, Shimano's <u>SR-3D</u> & <u>Fluidrive II Gear System</u> is a large-bore aluminum drive gear melded with proprietary coatings combined with specially shaped teeth that mesh with a hardened stainless steel pinion gear for optimal efficiency. These elements translate into strength, durability, smoothness, speed, leverage and power.

*Shimano's Propulsion Line Management System virtually eliminates the problems that plague spin casters; that is, line twist—often resulting in backlashes, wind knots, and very tangible tangles. The issue in virtually eliminated with their newly created spool-lip design, which allows for longer casts. This is not hype, attested to by Donna in a single exclamation, "Wow!" as she effortlessly sent her lure sailing above the suds—flawlessly—time and time again. The spool is cold forged aluminum with a ceramic coating for ultimate corrosion protection and scratch resistance. Its lip is ultra-hard stainless steel with a proprietary coating that reduces friction.

*Part and parcel to this propulsion system are insightful and innovative assists that thwart line twists: a stainless steel one-piece bail wire that reduces friction and makes quick work of aiding line to roller; an oversized power roller with an overflange that circumvents line memory; a redesigned bail trip mechanism working in conjunction with an S-Arm cam component to keep line in contact with the roller —a godsend in slack line situations whereby the line would invariably fall from the roller and back onto the bail wire. Too, the line roller features a Diamond-Like Carbon (DLC) coating, harder than titanium for overall smoothness.

*Aero Wrap II is a worm-gear system specifically designed to oscillate at optimal speed in relationship to its Line Management/Spool-Lip Propulsion System, offering the ultimate in uniformity with regard to line lay and winding shape.

***Salt W**ater Assist Stopper (not available on the SW 5000 model) is a back-up ratchet and pawl system that prevents high-speed damage to the one-way roller bearing that could result from water intrusion. However, *all* Stella SW models feature Super Stopper II, meaning that the roller has been beefed up to increase strength and durability. As all six Stella SW models feature the Super Stopper design in lieu of an anti-reverse switch, the likelihood of saltwater intrusion is virtually eliminated. It is the reason why Donna and I selected the 5000 SW and 8000 SW for the surf.

*Even the lightweight ergonomically designed egg-shaped non-slippery grip is well thought out, offering increased torque with tireless turns of the handle. You can truly feel the difference. Comfort and control are its distinguishing characteristics.

*Fourteen shielded stainless steel ball bearings (plus one roller bearing) for categorical corrosion and contaminant protection are but another hallmark of Stella's SW series of excellence. The ball bearings are protected by Shimano's A-RB (Anti-Rust Bearings) process, a procedure which makes them ten times more resistant to corrosion.

*Additionally, I relish Shimano's maintenance port feature that allows you to oil the interior mechanisms without having to disassemble the reel.

These are but a few of the many fine features found on these fabulous reels. You are definitely getting what you're paying for; manufacturer suggested retail price for the Stella 8000 SW is $830. The Stella 5000 SW runs $730. For Donna's and my needs, the 5000 SW and 8000 SW, respectively, are two pieces of artillery that will handle a variety of situations, including surfcasting applications.

Shakespeare's Ugly Stik spinning rods, paired with those exceptional reels, are what Donna and I feel offer well-balanced outfits. Matching these and other Shimano spinning reels to Shakespeare's Ugly Stik rods are listed below. But first let's examine another two spinning reels in our arsenal that fall between the extremes of medium and medium-heavy weapons of mass destruction. The prices drop considerably; not the quality or value. That's why I'm keeping you within the higher-end arena. Think Stella, Sustain, and Stradic, and you'll be thinking clearly.

**Bottom to top: Stella 8000 SW; Stella 5000 SW;
Sustain 5000 FE; Stradic 5000 FI**

Sustain FG & Stradic FJ Series

Note: As in Chapter 1, you'll select the current Sustain **FG** and Stradic **FJ** models in lieu of our Sustain FE and Stradic FI models. Keep in mind that our FE and FI models are the reels that Donna and I have field-tested and used for two to three seasons; in a word, flawless. Keep in mind, too, that the newer models reflect design refinements.

The new Sustain 5000 FG and Stradic 5000 FJ are two exceptional, mid-sized spinning reel models that fit a mid-range, medium-action mode. At a MSRP of $369.99 and $209.99, respectively, they cannot be beat for the simple reason that they offer virtually all the fine features of the Stella SWs, only in a smaller package. All told, there are seven models in each Sustain FG and Stradic FJ series from which to choose.

Those Sustain and Stradic 5000 models <u>do not</u> feature 14 ball bearings as with the Stella SW series. However, the Sustain 5000 FG model contains 8 shielded stainless steel ball bearings (plus one roller bearing) that have been put through the same <u>A-RB</u> process as the Stella series. The Stradic 5000 FJ model contains 5 shielded stainless steel ball bearings (plus one roller bearing) employing the same process, utilizing either rubber or stainless steel shields determined by bearing size. All told, the Sustain and Stradic series are superb spinning reels.

<u>Matching Medium/Heavy-Action Shimano Spinning Reel to Shakespeare's Ugly Stik Rod for Saltwater Applications</u>

Shimano Stella 8000 SW matched with Ugly Stik BWS 1100 12' 0" (3.60m) Action: Heavy (12-40 lb. test line) two piece; foam grip

<u>Matching Medium-Action Shimano Spinning Reel to Shakespeare's Ugly Stik Rod for Saltwater Applications</u>

Shimano Stella 5000 SW matched with Ugly Stik BWS 1100 8' 0" (2.40m) Action: Medium (10-25 lb. test line) two piece; foam grip

<u>Matching Medium-Action Shimano Spinning Reels to Shakespeare's Ugly Stik Rods for Saltwater and/or Significantly-Sized Freshwater Species</u>; e.g., lake trout, salmon, muskellunge, and the like:

Shimano Sustain 5000 FG matched with Ugly Stik SP 1101 7' 0" (2.13m) Action: Medium-Heavy (8-20 lb. test line) one piece; foam grip

Shimano Stradic 5000 FJ matched with Ugly Stik SP 1101 6'6" (1.98m) Action: Medium-Heavy (8-20 lb. test line) one piece; foam grip

Chapter 3

SELECTING HIGH QUALITY LIGHT TO MEDIUM/MEDIUM-HEAVY ACTION SALTWATER & FRESHWATER BAITCASTING REELS & MATCHING RODS

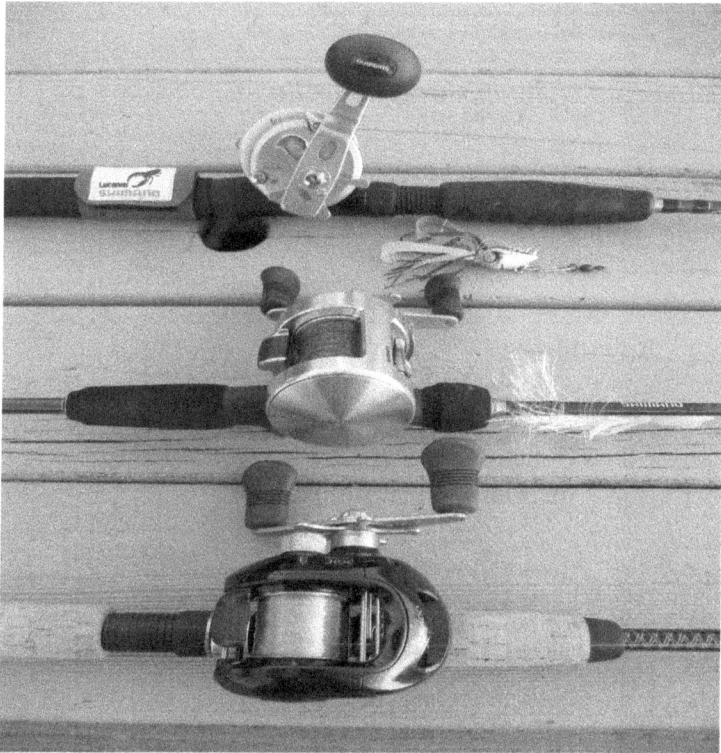

Top to Bottom: Shimano Calcutta TE 400 LJV;
Shimano Calcutta TE 401; Shimano Curado 301 E

As Donna and I truly enjoy sensitive rod action when fishing inshore for fluke, flounder (haven't seen too many of those of late) and porgies, we find that our short one piece 5½ foot medium-light action (10-17 pound test line) baitcasting Ugly Stiks, BWC 1121 model, are the ticket. A union of backbone, sensitivity and price are the hallmarks of these indestructible rods. Paired with conventional Penn 930 Levelmatics, lightweight (11.5 ounces) but gutsy baitcasting reels, this combination can and does take on denizens from the depths; namely, bass and blues. Fill a spool with braided line in lieu of monofilament and you have sensitivity personified. They are great outfits that are hard to beat for our bays.

Although Penn discontinued manufacturing their model 930 Levelmatic in

2004, having sold new for $100, they can still be purchased used (occasionally new) on eBay. As of this writing, they range in price from $45 to $85.

Here's the rub concerning Shakespeare's Ugly Stik model 1121 baitcasting rod. Try and find one. They are hard to come by but can be found. If you do locate this wand, you have gold in your hands. If you can't find one, then you must do the next best thing. Come as close as you can to matching this winner with another in terms of length, lure and line weight capability, quality Fuji guides, as well as the desired medium-light action. Good luck. Donna and I were, indeed, lucky. We found a pair of 1121s in a cluttered corner at Sports Authority. So hit the box stores and sporting good shops and do some digging. When surfing the Internet, you'll soon discover that other folks are searching for those rods, too. Don't ask me why rod and reel manufacturers discontinue such winners. I don't have the answer.

While searching for those proverbial needles in a haystack, I'm going to have you consider both expensive and more affordable baitcasting reels, matching them to bargain but quality rods.

If you have big bucks to spend on a true quality, low profile, lightweight, levelwind baitcasting reel for both salt and fresh water, you may want to consider Shimano's Calais [4 x 8] **D**igital **C**ontrol models: Calais 200 DC or 201 DC (right-hand, left-hand retrieve, respectively). This compact champ weighs in at 9.5 ounces and boasts 10 ball bearings plus one roller bearing. However, the MSRP is going to be a hard pill—don't choke—to swallow at $650. Perhaps some of us can offset this cost with, admittedly, a rationalization that I put forth in the first chapter covering Shimano's high-end spinning reels and Ugly Stik rods. The money you are absolutely going to save on a fine matching rod for Shimano's fantastic Calais **D**igital **C**ontrol reel just might justify the overall investment. Believe me when I tell you that *investment* is the operative word. Additionally, you are not going to have to search endlessly for a matching wand because Shakespeare's Ugly Stik, BWC 1120, medium-heavy action (12-20 lb. test line) winner is readily available in either a 6½ or 7-foot length. The rod sells for $38.68! I selected the 7-footer for more flexibility, which translates into better sensitivity. Combined with my Calais CL 201 DC, I can flip, pitch or cast lures a good distance without fear of endless backlashes. If you're familiar with baitcasting reels, you're probably asking yourself, "*How is that possible? Maybe if you had a very educated thumb to control spool speed*," you're probably concluding. The truth is that I can't wait to tell you exactly how!

Thirty-two distinct dial settings digitally control Shimano's Calais [4 x 8] braking system. **D**igital **C**ontrol [4 x 8]. What is it really? What does it do? In short, the Extreme Distance **X** Mode setting allows you to effortlessly cast great distances as when surfcasting or engaged in competition. The Long Distance **L** Mode immediately controls backlash by analyzing spool rotation. Next, the Accuracy **A** Mode braking system controls low-spool rotation speeds (as when pitching or skipping lures) and is designed to prevent overruns. Last but not least, the Wind **W** Mode applies the brakes throughout the entire cast, thwarting the spool from spinning faster than the lure can carry line when casting into a headwind.

Shimano Calais 200 DC [4 x 8] Baitcasting Reel

Each mode—**X~L~A~W**—is easily accessible via a hinged side plate. Additionally, an outer dial for eight separate brake-strength settings per mode is neatly positioned for instant fine-tuning. Hence, there are 32 [4 x 8] settings in all. Also, a cast knob makes for ultrafine tuning. It is Shimano's superior design and technology, brought about through many years of research and development, which make this braking system possible. The *brain* of the system is a self-charging, waterproof **D**igital **C**ontrol circuit that stores energy as you cast. Of course, there are other line control systems such as magnetic and centrifugal technology for less money. However, they require fuss work and fine adjustments that are best performed prior to fishing—not on the water—whereas Shimano's Calais **D**igital **C**ontrol system allows you to easily select a mode then dial a setting to instantly fine-tune the braking system while on the fly for varying conditions. Remarkably, the control system picks up an extra 10 to 15 thousand rpms than its conventional counterparts. Couple this feat with superior line control management and you have an extraordinary baitcasting reel. And, yes, it performs equally well with monofilament, fluorocarbon or braided line.

The reel's star drag system is intelligently designed; it is absolutely fast and unquestionably smooth. Applying the brakes with a maximum stopping power of 12 pounds, a retrieve ratio of 7.0:1, this is one serious tool for the suds or sweet water. It can handle anything from heavy spoons, poppers, crank baits, spinner baits to virtually weightless worms (plastic or otherwise). You are definitely getting what you are paying for. If you desire the ultimate in cast control, look no further for the finest low profile, lightweight, levelwind baitcasting reel on the planet!

For detailed information regarding the specific performance of each braking mode, visit fishshimano.com, or send for their catalog. It's a wealth of information.

Still can't justify spending $688.68 plus tax for the marriage of the ultimate reel and rod combination that I set forth? Admittedly, I won't blame you because it's not for everyone. It's for the fanatic who loves bait casting and would enjoy the versatility of this fantastic reel, which serves as a standard of excellence. The Calais 200 **DC** [4 x 8] is just that! I'll parallel it to such timepieces as a Patek Philippe, Vacheron Constantin, or Girard-Perregaux. Forget Rolex.

As the Calais **DC** 200 [4 x 8] is Shimano's latest innovation in digital control, the original **D**igital **C**ontrol braking system integrated in Shimano's **Calcutta TE DC** series (four models to choose from) can be had for a MSRP of $530. Although you will still have the benefit of eight levels of brake force, you will be giving up those four select modes: **X ~ L ~ A** and **W** across the braking curve as a result of the reels pre-programmed circuitry. This translates into the loss of efficient slow spool-speed rotation, essential when pitching or flipping lures. Too, the system limits extreme distance casting. For a savings of $120, ask yourself if it's worth the sacrifice. Serving as a fair to middling all-around curve, the original **DC** braking system cannot match the ingenious 'dial-your-desire' [4 x 8] **DC** model.

With a cost factor still in mind, you could put digital control innovation aside altogether and go with Shimano's Curado 300 E series, offered in either left- or right-handed models. It is a high performance reel boasting an ultra-smooth and powerful maximum drag setting of 15 pounds. That's some stopping power. The Dartainium drag system offers a wide range of settings.

Several features and specs include Shimano's High Efficiency Gearing (HEG); a lightweight but strong aluminum frame that houses an extra-deep aluminum spool capable of holding 240 yards of 12-pound test monofilament (approximate equivalent of 50-pound braid); 5 Shielded Stainless Steel Ball Bearings; 1 Shielded S A-RB (**A**nti-**R**ust **B**earing) Stainless Steel Ball Bearing; 1 A-RB Stainless Steel Roller Clutch Bearing (for a total of **7** bearings); 6.2:1 Gear Ratio; and 28 inches of line retrieve per crank. The reel weighs in at a mere 10.5 ounces, carrying an MSRP of $250. Again, please bear in mind that when I write up a product review, it is not simply field-tested over a weekend or two. The Curado E workhorse was put through a vigorous trial by ordeal over three seasons. Flawless would sum up this gutsy Shimano Curado bait caster.

Can't justify spending $250 for a fine baitcasting powerhouse reel in a lightweight package? Let's revert back to the rationalization tactic that I used in the first two chapters.

Matching the Curado E Baitcasting Reel to Rod

Quite frankly, you're wasting your money if you spend more than $50 on a baitcasting rod for the Curado 300 E. Shimano, Okuma, G. Loomis, St. Croix and Shakespeare Ugly Stick (spelled Stik) wands are rated as excellent baitcasting rods—but not necessarily in that order. However, all things being equal, the former four rods are priced far higher than a Shakespeare Ugly Stik. We're looking at double, triple and quadruple the price for a comparable rod. As you *generally* get what you pay for, folks automatically get talked into and/or simply reach for the more expensive rods. The fact is that the Ugly Stik is (again, all things being equal) tougher than other rods that cost considerably more. You may gain a bit more sensitivity and wield slightly less weight with more pricy rods, but they generally do not have the backbone of Shakespeare Ugly Stiks. Different strokes for different folks. Perhaps you can now justify putting the money that I hopefully saved you toward a superior Shimano Curado E 300 or 301 baitcasting reel.

In selecting a medium- medium-heavy action Ugly Stik baitcasting rod for the Curado 300 E, look for double-footed, chrome-plated stainless steel guides with aluminum oxide inserts and center bridges for extra support. Ugly Stiks simply can't be beat in terms of strength and durability. For the price, you will not likely find these superior type guides on other rods that command significantly higher price tags.

I couple the Curado 301 E (left-hand) reel to a single-piece Shakespeare BWC 1120 7' (2.13m) MH **M**edium-**H**eavy Action Ugly Stik rod (12–20 lb. test line). At the expense of mixing metaphors, I'm spooled with 120 yards of 20-pound test monofilament—loaded for bear. That's the approximate equivalent of 100-pound test braid.

Let's take an even closer look at some of the reel's other outstanding features. On the sideplate is a flip-key that easily accesses Curado's 300 E <u>Variable Brake System</u> (VBS) in order to quickly change weight adjustments and/or spools. The reason that the angler can cast extremely lightweight lures is in the design of the Magnumlite Spool. Creative construction coupled with innovative drilling techniques produces a light, thin-walled yet super-strong spool that offers ". . . the lowest start-up inertia *ever* in a Shimano reel," claims the company. With Curado's VBS friction adjustments, cast control is always under control. If you are experiencing a backlash with a particular lure, simply make the fine adjustment via the Variable Brake System, comprised of six brake weights, which can be changed by switching all or combinations of the weights. Easy to follow instructions come with the reel.

Opposite the access plate is the Cast Control knob to lessen or increase spool friction. Between the two friction control systems (the Variable Brake System and the Cast Control knob), backlashes [overruns] are virtually eliminated. If a backlash happens at the beginning of the cast, it is cleared by the Variable Brake System. If a backlash happens at the end of the cast, it is cleared by the Cast Control knob.

For instant hook-setting power, <u>Super Stopper II</u> anti-reverse employs a one-way stainless steel roller bearing to prevent backplay. Additionally, the Curado 300 E series features a backup system, <u>Assist Stopper</u>, utilizing an anti-reverse pawl and ratchet to positively eliminate failure. To paraphrase the company's claim, "Should the Super Stopper roller bearing fail to engage as the result of cold weather or over-lubrication, the Assist Stopper kicks in to provide a solid hookset the instant the roller bearing begins to slip. Most often, the angler will not even realize when this feature engages. By immediately stopping the backward rotation of the roller bearing, the Assist Stopper greatly reduces the chance of permanent damage to the Super Stopper, allowing the feature to continue to function as designed."

The <u>QuickFire II Clutch Bar</u> gives control of both spool and clutch with the touch of your thumb by either disengaging the spool or reengaging the gearing.

Curado's handlebar knobs are comfortable, made of Septon CPD, a thermoplastic elastomer that offers an appealing tactile feel. A round-headed five-spoke star drag is perfectly positioned behind the handlebar.

Note: For serious offshore angling, I'll address the Curado 300 E's big brother (the Curado 300 EJ), along with the Calcutta TE 400 LJV when we examine Shimano's unique Systems for jigging, subsurface, and top-water action in Chapter 18. The Calcutta TE 401 has been redesigned for 2013, presented as the new Calcutta D series, featuring X-Ship technology explained in Chapter 1. Too early for me to comment, except to say that Donna and I each own the older models, which can be paired with any of the medium/medium-heavy action rods covered. The reels comprise High Efficiency Gearing and are the hallmarks of fine craftsmanship. The MSRP on a new Calcutta 400 or 401 D is $379.99.

If price continues to be an issue, another reel manufacturer I'd consider is Abu Garcia. Abu Garcia was originally a watch manufacturer dating back to 1921. In the late 1930s, the company started manufacturing reels. No, I'm not making any comparisons to those fine timepieces mentioned earlier referencing the Calais 200 DC [4 x 8]. I make mention purely as a piece of trivia. However, keep in mind that you pretty much get what you pay for, so think high-end selection when choosing reels, be they fly, spin or bait casting. In the case of Abu Garcia, select from their high-end Ambassador (Ambassadeur) models ranging from $100 to $200.

An important word on right- or left-hand retrieve handles. On most fly and spinning reels, it's a rather simple procedure to convert from either right- or left-hand retrieve modes. On most fly reels, it's a matter of repositioning the pawl. Instructions generally cover this conversion. On most spinning reels, one can easily switch the handle from one side of the reel to the other. However, concerning *all* baitcasting reels, one must decide on either a right- or left-handed model from the onset, for there is no conversion option. Some reels only come right-handed. Occasionally, within a model series, several right-handed reels are offered whereas a left-handed option may be limited to a single choice. A word to the wise; be very careful in your selection.

I'm right-handed; yet, I purchased Shimano's left-hand model baitcasting reels because I'm more comfortable cranking the handle with my left hand. All my fly reels and spinning reels are set up for left-hand retrieve. Our Penn 930 Levelmatics—along with a pair of ancient Penn Senator baitcasting reels—came with right-hand retrieve. Fine for dropping a line over the rail or trolling, but for continual casting performance, I do not like changing hands in order to retrieve a lure. It's all a matter of preference.

Chapter 4

LEARNING & RELEARNING FLY CASTING

Employing the **KISS** principle (**K**eep **I**t **S**imple **S**ystem), I'll cut to the chase by separating the wheat from the chaff. For openers, I will clear away the cobwebs covering the alleged mysterious art of fly casting in four basic areas:

Demystifying the Alleged Arcane Art of the Long Rod

An Innovative Approach to Learning Fly-Casting

** Speed-Sink/Floating Lines for Salt Water **

Weight-Forward Floating Lines for both the Suds and Sweetwater

THE BASICS & BEYOND

The art of angling is a serene art. The art of fly-fishing is art personified. I started fly-fishing freshwater streams and rivers in western Long Island in the early sixties. Clad in hip boots or waders, I relied heavily on the flow of water from a stream or river to carry my level taper floating line, leader and fly to unsuspecting brookies, rainbows and an occasional brown trout, for I was not terribly adept at casting the artificial any notable distance. Years later, I purchased the then popular double taper floating line. No matter how hard I tried, even after paying heed and homage to fellow fly-fishermen who offered pointers and supposedly sound advice, I wasn't really getting anywhere. No matter how many brochures, pamphlets and books I perused, I was not gaining any significant ground. But for the time being, that was all right as I had the current to wend and carry my fly within striking range. It proved sufficient until I moved on to ponds and then lakes, fly-fishing from the shoreline. A good cast for me was forty feet—without a wind in my face. But there were times, more often than not, when I needed fifty feet or better because those telltale rings and ripples of feeding fish were almost always several yards beyond . . . my ability. So for the most part, out of sheer frustration, I limited my fly-fishing to rivers and streams.

As the years flew by, I spent many an hour spin or bait casting both fresh and salt water, sporadically returning to the edge of those trout-water ponds and tranquil lakes with fly rod back in hand—still with less than desired results. The years turned into decades. I almost always caught fish; fairly nice fish in fact. But I knew for certain that bigger beauties lay just out of my reach with the long rod, schooling up in the center of several deeper, cooler pools. Unless I was assisted by a moving stream or river, or maneuvering about a larger body of water in a rowboat or canoe, casting any respectable distance from a shoreline still proved a challenge. By then, I was learning that not all fly lines are created equal. There are four basic types: level taper, double taper, weight-forward taper, and shooting tapers—the latter of which are often generically lumped together and referred to as speed-cast tapers, full sinking lines, shooting heads or just plain heads. Herein lies the confusion, for not all shooting tapers are created equal either. Not by a long shot; pun intended. Therefore, for the sake of clarity, I will specifically cast a keen light and address shooting tapers as speed-sink/floating lines for saltwater situations. Too, I shall address weight-forward floating lines for saltwater and freshwater applications; but first things first.

I had initially been sold on the idea, literally, that a level or a double taper fly line was the way to go. Reputedly, they have their application in freshwater fly-fishing; they are, I feel, of little use in salt water, especially when weighed against the advantages of a weight-forward line as such, be it fished in either fresh water or the brine. From the very moment I set aside my level and double taper lines and topped off the reel with a weight-forward line, I noticed something remarkable on my first cast. I immediately, although subtly, began to *feel* and then finally realize what those brochures, pamphlets, books and fellow fly-fishermen had been talking about; that is, loading the rod, timing and technique. Suddenly, I was casting another ten to fifteen feet further than ever before. I wanted to experiment with other lines. However, fly lines were and are expensive, particularly for a person of modest means. It is not like buying a spool of monofilament or even braided line. Furthermore, a heavier line would necessitate a heavier rod. That was simply prohibitive at the time. Therefore, I stayed with my 6-weight rod and matching 6 weight-forward floating fly line for many years.

When Donna and I first moved out to eastern Long Island, we fished the estuaries and bays with light spinning and baitcasting tackle as I had done as a young man. One morning, I wet a line and fished a stretch of river near our home with that perfectly balanced 6-weight rod outfit, modifying the setup with, of course, a heavier leader and larger fly. The rod and reel proved less than adequate for some of the big blues I was hooking, so I finally graduated to a well-balanced 8-weight setup with a large arbor reel for greater line capacity.

Without a doubt, I was casting a few feet further because of the heavier fly line. I could see and feel the difference between the 6-weight outfit that I had been using for years and the new 8-weight. Years later, a few weakfish in the six- to eight-pound category along with several respectable stripers as well as a mess of monster blues, tipping the Toledo at seventeen-plus pounds, convinced me to upgrade to a 10-weight outfit. But as I was moving into deeper waters, I chose an intermediate sink-tip line in order to get down into the water column. I began researching, in depth, considerably heavier speed-sink/floating fly lines. Virtually all of its weight is integrated within the front section of the line, which can range from some twenty to thirty feet on average. Step up one or two sizes from the rod's recommended line weight and—believe me—you will immediately fathom what loading a rod is *really* all about; that is, the momentary storing of energy upon the backcast. I wish I had that experience very early on, for I would have grasped the principles of fly casting in a heartbeat. Practicing first in the backyard, my heart raced the moment I lifted the line from the ground into a backcast, then came forward and effortlessly shot some forty feet of line with such energy that it tore from the reel and sounded the drag. I knew that if I had let fifty feet of line drape before my feet, it would have carried forward with gusto, too. I was hooked, figuratively speaking.

The next cast incorporated two false casts; that is, a forward cast in which the line is not released but kept airborne with a back-and-forth motion. Fifty-plus feet flew sharply forward, without even employing a single haul (a steady, quick pull with the line hand on the backcast). Wow! I felt that I was on my way to stardom, and for the very first time, I should add. Then on to perfecting the double-haul (steady, quick pulls with the line hand on both the back and forward false casts). More on those two speed strokes later. I could now *feel*, without a doubt, what was supposed to take place with regard to timing and technique. It was something that I had never before quite nailed down. It was not accomplished overnight. No, sir. No, ma'am. It took me days of practice to get the rhythm down pat, whereas before, I hadn't managed to execute those fine points in decades. In a matter of months, I was casting eighty to ninety feet. Not consistently, but I was getting there. However, in taking my newfound knowledge from the lawn to the suds initially proved quite another matter.

The conventional casting, retrieving and instantaneous recasting technique in utilizing a roll cast (a forward cast with the line upon the water without employing a backcast) with a floating line simply did not work on the water while employing a speed-sink/floating line. In the yard, where I could pick up and quickly recast a good section of line with ease, the heavier head did not function in the same fashion upon the suds simply because the weighty line would immediately sink and stay sunk . . . along with my hopes of becoming similarly proficient as on land. Of course, I could have just left well enough alone and hauled in the head to within a few feet of the rod tip, employed another false cast, working the section out to the balance point before shooting the line anew. After all, I was only sacrificing efficiency in terms of the speed of a roll cast for the coveted distance I demanded. But somehow that was not quite good enough as I've often been accused of wishing to lead a charmed life. What to do? It became clear that more research was on the horizon. It took a little time to learn the science of overcoming gravity with a sinking line. I will share that technique with you in just a moment.

As there are, indeed, a ton of shooting lines on the market, what my research regarding the subject primarily boiled down to was learning to keep the weighted front section of a shooting taper airborne before sending it into the next county. No problem there. I had the desired distance-cast down pat. I wasn't even concerned about accuracy . . . yet. It was all a matter of degree, working a specified length of line with what I could handle comfortably. For that reason, I started with a twenty-four foot shooting section, eventually moving up to thirty feet.

Ostensibly, shooting lines seem and feel difficult to handle for a good number of people. There is little wonder why many fly-fishing folks, newcomers as well as some veterans, shy away from those shooting tapers, for the technique of moving a sinking line through the air does not work the same way as conventional weight-forward floating fly lines. Thank goodness for people like Lefty Kreh who can sum up and resolve that problem in a single sentence as in one of his books, *Fly Fishing in Salt Water.* "You want to throw as slow a cast behind you as possible, and here's the catch—with a wide loop," the world renowned fly-fishing author and caster instructs. This is the antithesis of what we learn when casting conventional (floating) fly lines, be it level, double-taper or weight-forward, which calls for a fast backcast and a tight loop. Learning to alter that cast with a shooting taper will pay dividends in terms of distance. Considerable distance. After the loop opens up behind you, meaning that it is now laid out straight, you proceed with your forward cast as you ordinarily would.

Still, we are not out of the woods. Off the lawn for certain, but not off that body of water that beguiled me earlier with regard to the roll cast because that line, once again, is back to sinking steadily in the suds. It is evident that you do not have the resistance (drag) as with a floating line upon the water's surface to load the rod again. Hence, the 'water haul' cast to the rescue.

A water haul is a cast that lends drag so as to load the rod *slowly* but deeply. It is attained by deliberately retrieving the line and creating a modified roll cast, unlike a conventional roll cast. In other words, an altered roll-cast pickup is required in order to overcome the heavy line's resistance beneath the water. This is achieved by steadily drawing the sinking portion of the fly line (be it a twenty- or thirty-foot length) up to the rod tip and immediately lifting and executing a roll cast. However, when the very end of the sinking section clears the surface, a *slow* (unlike the conventional quick, strong pull) roll cast is executed. Keep in mind that slow and steady wins the race. Just like those false casts—with that wide loop in lieu of a tight one as stated above—this is precisely what you want to achieve on the backcast when you execute a roll cast. Similarly, when the loop opens up behind you, you make your conventional forward cast. With a little practice, you will find that weight-forward sinking lines are just as easy to cast and roll cast as weight-forward floating lines, while offering greater distance. That in itself, when fishing open bays and the ocean, is a significant plus if you are to cover as much water as possible in order to up your ante, which is precisely what you want to do unless specifically sight casting to your prize. Distance *and* accuracy may well be the order of the day.

As mentioned earlier, there are several sectional lengths of shooting tapers incorporated into a sinking/floating fly line. Generally speaking, fly lines run ninety to a hundred feet in length, while the sinking portion of a shooting taper, on average, is thirty feet for the suds. There are, for example, 20, 22, 24, 30, 35, 40 and even 45-foot sinking sections of 60 to 120-plus-foot fly lines, many with sink rates ranging from 3.75 ips (inches per second) to 10 ips on average. I would strongly recommend a 24-foot length shooting taper for openers before graduating to 30 feet. The sink rate, of course, depends on the type of fishing as well as the waters you are covering. There are several good saltwater fly lines on the market, inclusive of those shooting tapers. I have purchased Cortland, Orvis, Scientific Anglers, and Teeny fly lines, to name but a few.

Teeny fly lines offer a wide range of choices. Their T-Series and TS-Series in 24 and 30 feet, respectively, are fine places to start. Teeny's magic is in the marriage of a floating line matched to a sinking taper. All one piece. No knots. No splicing. No hinging (overhang that destroys the cast by sending a series of shockwaves through the line). Two colors determine Teeny's balance point, so there is no guesswork in where to draw and shoot the line. When the second color extends approximately one foot past the rod tip, it is magic time. And when it comes to cutting through a wind, which is the bane of many a saltwater fly-fisherman, shooting this type of line through a blow is simply a breeze.

In past years, through the Cornell Cooperative Extension, Donna and I have instructed fly casting for the Women's Outdoor Weekend Program at the 4-H Club in Riverhead, New York. Initially, in working with several students, I had used the traditional method of instruction, utilizing a balanced 6-weight freshwater outfit; specifically, a 6-weight graphite rod along with a matching 6-weight-forward floating line. I met with a modicum of success. Granted, I only had those newcomers for a couple of hours, teaching them the basics, then encouraging them to seek professional instruction and to practice, practice, practice.

In subsequent years, I continued in the same fashion; however, at a midway point in the lesson, I introduced a 6-weight graphite rod with a Teeny T-Series, T-300, 24-foot shooting head. When my students now loaded the rod, false casting twice or thrice while working the second color a foot past the front guide, then shot the line, the only thing that hinged were their jaws. They did not want to let go of nor go back to that *other rod*, but I insisted. By way of analogy, I explain to students that I first want them to learn the fundamentals of driving a stick shift automobile before having them handle an automatic. This way, they will be better prepared to handle both freshwater and saltwater situations, that is, casting a floating line for a delicate presentation or shooting a heavier sinking taper to cover distance as well as getting down into the water column.

It was not long before my students fully understood and aptly began to apply the basics. Why? Because they now had a fairly good idea of what those two rods and lines are supposed to do. One young woman finished her lesson by casting approximately forty feet with the conventional weight-forward floating line then threw approximately sixty feet with the rod set up with the shooting taper. She was positively thrilled with her performance. Through the years, I have had the opportunity to work with many students who simply wanted to learn the basics while others were interested in improving their fly-fishing skills. I alternate between conventional weight-forward floating lines and shooting tapers in order to teach timing and technique.

Employing a shooting taper one, two or even three sizes up from the recommended rod weight (for purposes of demonstration) will instantly give the newcomer the feel and confidence required to load a rod properly. Practice on land first before hitting the water. Too, tie an orange or yellow piece of yarn (about three inches in length) to the end of a short leader of about two feet. After only a few false casts—with a slow back-and-forth motion—you will almost instinctively know that it is too heavy to backcast with force, for you will surely run amuck, sending shockwaves through the line and causing turmoil. I want you hooked on the positive concept of a shooting taper, not pinned in the pants. So don't push the envelope. Nice and easy does it. After you get the feel—and feel the power that, indeed, you will—release approximately a foot or two of line at a time on both the forward and backcast as you work up to the end of the shooting section. This will help you learn timing and technique, building confidence as you deliver your forward cast.

Try to work to a point employing only two false casts before shooting your line forward. Later, as promised, I'll cover the single and double haul in detail in order for you to gain greater distance. You do not have to have these latter two skills mastered in order to move from the lawn to the suds, just as surely as you do not have to nail down the water haul in order to nail and haul in fish. But broadening your horizons will certainly add to your enjoyment in the wonderful sport of fly-fishing. The idea is to have fun. Take things one step at a time. *Slowly.* That's the key. The distance offered by utilizing shooting tapers will put you miles ahead of the game. Do not sell shooting lines short. With a little practice, you will find that they are long on performance.

Below are a number of tips to keep in mind that will positively make you a far better fly caster whether you are throwing weight-forward floating lines or shooting tapers. Although I am advocating shooting tapers for learning the *feel* of loading a rod, I am by no means dismissing or downplaying weight-forward floating lines, for they are essential in both freshwater and saltwater applications. As a matter of fact, the initial points I'll be addressing pertain to weight-forward floating lines unless otherwise indicated. You will do well by learning to handle both lines.

The following step-by-step tips have been strategically arranged and dispensed in digestible doses so as not to overwhelm the newcomer. They are your prescription for success. The more advanced student need only scan the list. The beginner should, of course, heed the advice and practice the art at his or her own pace. Fly casting is not a black art but rather a most enjoyable and rewarding skill to master. Much like a golf swing, fly casting combines timing and technique. Unlike the game of golf, you may take that *shot* over again—and without penalty!

Remember, we are beginning with a weight-forward floating line.

1. Before making your first cast of the day—whether employing a weight-forward floating line or a shooting taper—pull the fly line from the reel. Run the line firmly through a soft dry rag so as to straighten the coils. This will facilitate the cast.

2. As if you were shaking hands, hold and place your thumb atop the cork handle, slightly in back of where it joins the rod.

3. If you are right-handed, step forward with your left foot, taking up a comfortable position. If you are left-handed, step forward with your right foot.

4. While practicing in the yard, straighten out any slack line in front of you before making the backcast. You must get the end of the line moving before you can make a decent cast.

5. Much has been written on the "clock system" regarding where to begin the backcast and when to shoot the line on the forward cast. Some instructors subscribe to the overhead one o'clock and ten o'clock positions, respectively. It doesn't much matter if it's a. m. or p. m. Yes, I'm making a joke. On a more serious note, forget the "clock system" of casting altogether because there are just too many variables at work: types of fly lines, rod tapers, size of flies employed, even your body-build. The clock system method of casting has confounded matters greatly. World famous fly-casting instructor Lefty Kreh couldn't agree more. "Clocks are for telling time," he makes quite clear with a big smile. Of course, sight-casting for a fish as a means of verbally establishing direction ("Bone fish at three o'clock," your partner or guide could announce), or casting around the face of a clock as a tool for learning wind situations are altogether different because we are then referring to a clock on a horizontal plane.

6. Instead of wielding the fly rod back-and-forth in a relatively stiff and restricted vertical (overhead) position, you will be learning—or relearning—to cast in a more comfortable fashion, away from your body, loading the rod and executing strokes at an approximate 45-degree angle for starters. You are in no way sacrificing speed or power. As a matter of fact, you will be gaining in these departments because the longer you move the rod through an arc, the greater the cast. Keep in mind that some casts may even be made on a 90-degree plane. Not only is this method more relaxing, it is by far safer, for the fly is away from your face. So, once again, do not get locked into the "clock system" approach.

7. Begin by working with whatever length of line you can manage. Keep your rod low and relatively parallel to the ground, then (with command) lift the straightened length of line off the ground, sending it rearward—stopping abruptly. For starters, count to two in order to give the line loop time to straighten out (unroll) behind you before making your forward cast. You cannot make a good forward cast without first making a good backcast.

8. Because it may be difficult to see what's going on with the line behind you, it would be helpful if you had someone to tell you when that line loop has unrolled. This will help get your timing and technique down pat.

9. Now, with the line unrolled behind you, come forward with your rod hand, stopping sharply just as the rod passes your body, pointing the rod tip at eye level toward (not necessarily at) the target. When on the water, cast the line at eye level (toward the horizon), not down at the water where it will make an unnecessary splash and frighten fish.

10. Let's fine-tune those two casts. Start the backcast while keeping your wrist, forearm and elbow at shoulder height and on a plane parallel to the ground. Lefty Kreh refers to this as "the shelf." Use your forearm to make the casts. Do not twist your wrist. However, know that bending your wrist (along with two other elements to be covered later) determines loop size.

11. Speed up and stop on the back and forward cast when employing weight-forward floating lines. Conversely, take it nice and easy on the back and forward cast when employing shooting tapers.

12. Press your thumbnail slightly down at the end of the forward cast to avoid what is called tailing loops, inaccurately referred to as wind knots. This prevents the line and leader from crashing into one another and causing a knot.

13. After making the forward cast, do not drop the rod tip down to the fishing position until the end of the line has passed the tip by a rod's length, otherwise you will widen the loop and shorten your casting distance.

14. Keep in mind that the line goes in the direction that the rod tip speeds up and stops. On the backcast, with acceleration being applied, you do not see where the rod tip actually stops. But try and picture where that rod tip is winding up if you suddenly apply the brakes in the vertical position on that backcast. The rod tip is traveling back and then down, creating a sag in the line. This you do not want. Therefore, now send your backcast angled slightly upward in a sort of stabbing motion. This will enable the line to straighten out behind you so that you may now make a forward cast without the loss of energy needed to properly load the rod.

15. Speed-ups and sudden stops on the backward and forward casts create tight loops, which is what you want to achieve when employing weight-forward floating lines.

16. The shorter the distance you speed up and stop, the tighter the loop. The faster you speed up and stop over that short distance, the further the line will travel.

17. Pretend you're throwing the fly line at the tip of the rod. This will help you form tighter loops when employing a weight-forward floating line.

18. There are a plethora of casts that a person can learn. A most useful cast is the roll cast that we spoke about earlier while employing a speed-sink/floating taper. However, when employing a lighter weight-forward floating line, you will need the resistance (drag) of a body of water. Therefore, let us purposely pick a spot on a stream or river where we would be impeded from making a backcast because of a backdrop of bushes or trees. With a length of line lying in the water before you, start by lifting and bringing (not casting) the rod well in back of you, taking up any slack in the line. You are now loading the rod by creating surface tension because the water is grabbing the line. Stop! Immediately, sweep the rod forward to a point adjacent to your body and sharply execute your roll cast with a speed-up and sudden stop. Watch the line rocket forth.

Note: In short order, you will instinctively learn to load the rod and shoot line when employing either weight-forward floating lines or speed-sink/floating tapers. A bit of practice coupled with fine-tuning, and you will discover those sweet spots.

19. After a day of fishing, whether in salt water or fresh water, clean your line with warm water and a mild detergent by gently running it through a wet, soapy, soft rag. Rinse and dry. Occasionally, with a soft rag, apply a fly line dressing recommended by the manufacturer. This will polish, protect and facilitate casting weight-forward floating lines as well as speed-sink/floating tapers. As you did with your fly line, clean your rod and reel with warm water and a mild detergent; wipe clean and dry. Simply hosing off a rod and reel does not rid them of salt and grime.

Advanced Instruction: The Single and Double Haul

Single Haul

1. Learn the single haul with a weight-forward floating line. After you have your backcast and forward cast down pat, easily throwing some 40-plus feet of line, you are now ready to achieve greater distance casting by adding additional speed to the stroke. Start with 20 feet of line out, working in increments of 5 feet until you lose control. Cease, halt, and desist. That means stop. Strip in that last five feet of line, and start again. Continue with a few false casts. As you begin your last backcast, pull (not jerk) the line sharply yet smoothly and steadily downward (about a foot) and away from your body as you bring the rod forward to shoot the line. Feel the added power? The single haul will increase both line speed and rod load.

    a) Fine-tune this cast by pivoting your body 45 degrees rearward as you begin to haul.

b) Control the shooting line with your line hand by forming a loose O-ring with the tip of your forefinger and thumb, through which the line shall easily pass. Practice the single haul until you are proficient.

Double Haul

1. As with the single haul, learn the double haul with your weight-forward floating line. After you have practiced and mastered the single haul, you are now ready for speed and distance personified. Hence, the double haul. As you execute a single haul, the line hand fades upward to be in a position to haul a second time as you make the forward cast. Timing is crucial and must be practiced. Here are the keys: As the line hand is raised upward to be in position for the second haul, you should *feel* and *feed* the line pull in that direction, that is, upward. Start the rod hand motion a fraction of a second before you start the line hand. You should feel the speed and power in executing both strokes.

 a) Fine-tune this powerful speed cast by concentrating on your hand movements. As a gauge, run and keep your line taut between your reel and the first stripper guide (guide closest to the handle). Your hauls are approximately 6 inches. The line hand should be within a foot of the reel. Hands are close together on the backcast, apart on the forward-downward pull; hands come close together on the backcast, apart on the forward-downward pull; hands come close together on the backcast, apart on the forward-downward pull—shoot the line. In short order, you will have added a turbocharger to your casting stroke. Did you remember to turn your body? Did you remember those sudden stops on both the backward and forward cast that you learned earlier?

 b) On the final backcast, allow the line, rod, and hands to stop then fade back a bit farther for an even longer, more powerful cast. Hands come apart on the forward-downward pull; hands close together on the backcast, apart on the forward-downward pull; sudden stop—shoot the line.

 c) "Ah, but when do I shoot the line on the final forward cast for maximum distance?" is the often asked question. And the answer is: "When you see the line loop roll forward of the tip of your rod." It is a matter of timing and must be practiced.

 d) For still a bit more added distance, on the final forward cast, turn the rod and reel inward toward your body.

 e) Whether employing a speed-sink/floating taper or a weight-forward floating line, it is important to keep in mind that once the heavier section passes through the rod tip by approximately a foot or two, there is a loss of control because the portion of the line outside the rod tip is now too heavy to support the thinner, lighter line behind it. Where is a fly line's perfect balancing point before the allowable overhang (hinging) destroys your cast? There is no guesswork in determining a Teeny line's sweet spot. My Teeny 90-foot #8 weight-forward floating line's magic moment occurs when the second color escapes the rod tip at 37 feet.

 f) Lastly, it is <u>most important</u> to note that once you false cast to this perfect balance point—regardless of the line manufacturer, irrespective of whether the line is a weight-forward floating line or a speed-sink floating taper—this backcast becomes your final backcast and necessitates your shooting the line on the forward cast. If you can effectively manage aerializing the heavier section of a given fly line to a foot or two beyond the point where the line would overhang; i.e., *hinge*, you are on your way to casting the entire line, be it 80, 90, or 100-plus feet.

Note: Only after you have mastered both the single and double haul with a weight-forward floating line should you graduate to a speed-sink/floating taper, its sinking section not to exceed 20 to 24 feet. Later, you may wish to work up to a 30- to 35-foot sinking section.

Lefty Kreh makes a fine point by saying that we should *not* learn to cast like Lefty Kreh—or any instructor. What we need to do is learn from them the basic principles of fly casting. Learning how a fly line behaves in a series of situations is what is going to transform you into a fine fly caster. Therefore, I have studied the techniques of those who I believe to be among some of the finest fly casters and/or instructors on the planet: folks like Billy Pate, Barry and Cathy Beck, Doug Swisher, Chico Fernandez, Ed Jaworowski, and, of course, Lefty Kreh. I have brought you the basics and beyond by discriminately adding and subtracting what I believe will leave you with lessons that will increase your understanding and enjoyment.

To add to that pleasure, I strongly advise the beginner right on through the advanced fly caster to join a fly-fishing club in his or her area; this translates into a hands-on experience from which you will benefit greatly. Eastern Flyrodders of Long Island, New York, is a club that Donna and I had belonged to for many years before it left the Riverhead area. Clubs as such create an invaluable body of knowledge that covers virtually every aspect of the sport. You'll find several references listed under the Resource section.

In the following chapter, I will cover Fly Rods, Reels, Lines, Backing, Leaders and Tippets in detail. If you are new to this wonderful sport and feel that you might want to try your hand at fly-casting—not yet having purchased equipment and materials—you are going to save a bundle of money without sacrificing quality. If you are already set up, you may want to consider a second fly rod and reel as a backup. When on the water, it would be ideal to have one rod and reel at the ready to cast a weight-forward floating line, the other a speed-sink/floating taper.

Chapter 5

SELECTING QUALITY LIGHT TO MEDIUM/MEDIUM-HEAVY ACTION SALTWATER & FRESHWATER FLY RODS & MATCHING REELS

Rods, Reels, Backing, Lines, Leaders and Tippets

I'll begin by saying that the products presented throughout this chapter will save you a bundle of money. They have been tried, tested and are proven winners. They are quality items that offer the consumer a high level of performance at a price that won't send the purchaser to the poorhouse. They have been put through the rigors of a marine environment, subjected to many a sea trial on numerous fishing trips by experts in the field as well as yours truly. They have been placed into the hands of veterans and novices alike. In some cases, at day's end, the products had to be pried from the grips of students, neighbors, friends and acquaintances. No, this account is not akin to *Consumer Reports*. It is, however, a reliable wellspring of information based on hands-on operations, sound observations and common sense. Additionally, the suggestions and advice set forth here are based on a single principle. **KISS: K**eep **I**t **S**imple **S**ystem. Once we start making things too complicated, we wind up omitting an important ingredient from the recipe of success, if not life in general. So let's not forget to factor in what recreational fishing is really all about. Fun. If we have to be convinced and told this twice, thrice or more times, then we must reinforce that solid principle by reminding ourselves and adhering to equation number two, which some folks refer to as **K**eep **I**t **S**imple **S**tupid. I think you get the drift. So, let's immediately consider two fine fly rods that positively make the grade for saltwater and freshwater fly-fishing applications, covering most angling situations.

Fly Rods

My first choice for a quality entry level freshwater fly rod or as a second backup rod is a **Temple Fork Outfitters (a.k.a. TFO) Lefty Kreh Signature Series Model 0690-2 piece, 6-Weight—with aluminum double uplocking reel seat.**

My first choice for a quality entry level saltwater fly rod, or as a second backup rod is a **TFO-Lefty Kreh Signature Series Model 1090-2 piece, 10-Weight—with aluminum double uplocking reel seat and fighting butt.**

Both are Clearly Quality-Value Winners.
In 2004, I upgraded to a quality Temple Fork Outfitters 10-weight fly rod.

Today, the rod is retailing for $119.95. No, this is not a typographical error. Specifically, this value-winner is a translucent dark green nine foot, two piece, IM6 graphite, Lefty Kreh Signature Series One rod, manufactured by Temple Fork Outfitters, with full wells grip and fighting butt. The rod's progressive taper loads fast and has the power and punch to deliver fantastic line speed and distance. To quote Joe Cravotta (former owner and operator of Parkwood Outfitters in Bohemia, Long Island), "The days of the multi-hundred dollar fly rods are over," unless, of course, you insist on spending big bucks. Is it necessary to do so in order to receive caliber-class craftsmanship and performance? Absolutely not. At a price that can't be beat, the model 1090-2 piece 10-weight rod is a midrange workhorse for fishing the brine.

If I had to purchase but a single fly rod for our freshwater streams and ponds, it would be a TFO 0690-2 piece; that is, a Temple Fork Outfitters Lefty Kreh Signature Series 6-weight, 9 foot 2-piece IM6 Graphite wand weighing 3.9 ounces—for an outstanding price of $109.95. Period—end of story.

I have well over a dozen fly rods, some of which are outrageously priced. I need not tell some of you what you can expect to pay for names like Winston, Sage, G. Loomis, Scott, and Orvis. Just as sure as God made little green apples, you would pay hundreds of dollars more than the prices cited. Some of those *other* long rods should be mortgaged by retail merchants in lieu of being sold outright. Hyperbole aside, those rod makers have their work cut out for them in terms of justifying their high prices against the high quality and affordable costs of Temple Fork's spectacular selection of Lefty Kreh Signature Series fly rods; from a 2-weight on up to a 14- through 17-weight. TFO's gamut runs from light freshwater to heavy-duty sea sticks, making it crystal clear that there is certainly a Temple Fork rod to meet your specific needs.

Temple Fork fly rods are endorsed by such names as Gary and Wanda Taylor, Ed Jaworowski, and, of course, Lefty Kreh. I have field tested these rods under some rather adverse conditions. A fly rod on a boat can sometimes take a beating no matter how careful we are. All hardware within the Series for which the rod was designed is top-notch—fore to aft—with large, comfortable fighting butts on the heavier weight rods. These TFO rods are simply outstanding, backed by a no-fault warranty for the life of the original registered owner. Return a damaged rod with $25 to cover shipping and handling, and you're back on the water.

Keeping things simple for sampling the suds, you do not need a heavier rod than a 10-weight outfit. An 8-weight would even be adequate for most situations. Keep in mind that a heavy rod will tire you out quickly. Tearing the above down to basics, I'll strongly suggest either a TFO 0890, 8-weight, or a 1090 10-weight. Both models are two-piece, nine foot IM6 graphite with aluminum two-ring uplocking reel seats and fighting butts. For $120, how can you go wrong? You can't. You won't. These two rods will cover most of your saltwater situations. It is the perfect place to start—and perhaps even finish.

An appropriate all-around fly rod for fishing our freshwater streams, ponds and lakes is a TFO 6-weight wand. It will get the job done quite nicely whether handling brookies, rainbows or brown trout. If you are going to ply the waters for panfish such as bluegills and perch, play around with a light 4-weight rod.

That's it in a nutshell. We don't have to, nor shall we, make things complicated. Let's move on to suitable matching reels.

Trion Series Pflueger Fly Reels
Models 1990 & 1912 Large Arbor Designs

I married my TFO 10-weight 1090 rod to a Pflueger Trion, model 1990, machined aluminum large arbor spool. As a point of information, I have well over a dozen fly reels ranging from expensive to inexpensive: Abel, Albright, Crystal River, Orvis, Pflueger, Scientific Anglers, and Shakespeare. For a total cost of $250 for the TFO 10-weight 1090 rod ($120) coupled with the Pflueger Trion model 1990 reel (approximately $130), it is an incredible setup in terms of both quality and value. Of course, if you want to lay out well over six bills for an Abel Super Series 8, or some other fine reels such as Billy Pate, Lamson, and Tibor, withholding their true costs from the other half of the household, well, what can I say? I might be fishing your body from the bay one day.

Like my Abel Super 8 fly reel, the Pflueger Trion Series is machined from bar stock aluminum; anodized and highly polished. The Trion Series has oversized ball bearings and a center-disc drag system for good control. The drag, in essence, is what you're paying for. Whereas Abel's drag system boasts 'Stop-A-Sub' reliability, my Pflueger Trion model 1990 can and has brought big brutes to a screeching halt.

I was so impressed with my Trion model 1990 (spool diameter of 3¾ inches) it was not long before I purchased Trion's model 1912 (spool diameter 41/8 inches), which according to the specifications chart can hold 250 yards of 30-pound test backing—up to a 12-weight, double-taper floating line. The Trion model 1990 holds 100 yards of 20-pound test backing—up to a 10-weight forward line.

Once again, keeping in accordance with the KISS principle, I firmly believe that these two Pflueger Trion Series models can tackle just about anything in our inshore waters. The model 1912 will run you approximately $160. Extra spools for the 1990 and 1912 are about $60 and $70, respectively. Short of heading down to the Keys for *big* tarpon or billfish, or further south, say Belize to Costa Rica for *giant* tarpon, billfish and other species that would accept a fly, I trust that the drag system on these two models will not leave you in the lurch in plying our local waters. If you're truly out hunting for trophy game fish, that's an entirely different story. You will want, and you'll pay dearly for a stalwart reel with a darling of a drag; otherwise, you're sure to be a sorry sort. But for our coastal waters, generally speaking, playing big bass, monster blues, albies and such with these Trion Series large arbor reels will prove more than satisfactory.

Keeping things very simple, lock a model 1990 Trion Series Pflueger fly reel onto your Temple Fork model 1090 10-weight fly rod, and get ready for some serious fun.

Fly-Reel Backing

For backing, I prefer Cortland's Dacron or Micron in 20- and 30-pound test:

the former for smaller arbor fly reels set up for freshwater species; the latter for larger arbor reels set up for saltwater species. Thirty-pound test backing is a good insurance policy against abrasion. In order to properly spool the correct amount of line onto a fly reel, it is advisable to reverse the entire procedure. That is, start with a leader attached to the arbor; attach the fly line (thicker diameter first), followed by the backing; finally, wind the line (evenly) to fill the reel to near capacity (leaving approximately ¼ inch of space from around the rim of the reel). You now have the proper amount of line. Next, remove the backing carefully (preferably upon an empty spool so that you don't *wind* up with a mess), followed by the fly line and leader. Making the appropriate connections (knots and loops) is better left to the shopkeeper the first time out, for there are several approaches. Later, you can easily learn these techniques from a book or video. Personally, I prefer whipped-loop connections. They are, indeed, strong and allow you to readily change fly lines to backing and leaders to fly lines.

Speed Tapers vs. Weight-Forward Floating Lines for Salt Water

I wish I could tell you, *precisely*, what fly line for a particular rod would best suit your individual needs. The fact is I can't. Not without first knowing the answer to at least half a dozen questions. And only then would I be able to give you ballpark figures. The right church, wrong pew type of scenario would probably prevail. The simple reason being is that it's all too complicated in that there are several variables to consider, which tend to compound matters and therefore cloud reasoning.

Of course, you have certain guidelines. Your rod will indicate what weight line to use. The problem is that not all rods and lines are created equal. Then again, there are rules of thumb. "Go up two line weights; especially with that shooting head," you'll hear folks suggest. "That Redington rod can handle it." Huh! Is that well-meaning person aware that you're casting a looped component five-foot slow-sink mini-tip, a twelve-foot intermediate section, or perhaps a twenty- to thirty-foot integrated speed-cast shooting taper? Are the terms shooting heads, sinking shooting-heads, and traditional shooting or speed-cast tapers used interchangeably? Should they be? Do the grain weights of fly lines accurately correspond to their sink rates in inches per second? Is the timing and casting technique employed with lengthy sinking lines or speed-sink/floating lines the same as with conventional weight-forward floating lines? Should I even bother with level or double-taper fly lines in saltwater applications? The answers to those six questions are, respectively: probably not; quite often; no; no; no; and lastly (in my opinion), absolutely not.

Keep in mind a single truth and you'll begin to understand the complexity of the above. There is no industry standard in matching the grain weight of fly lines to unilaterally correspond with its sink rate. Each manufacturer applies its own rating system—at best, placing a particular line within a category to cover a range of rod weights. For example, a Teeny TS-Series 450 sinking line has a sink rate of 8 ips (inches per second). That translates into the sinking portion of the line; in other words, the first 30 feet, weighing 450 grains, covering a range of rod weights from 9 through 12. Realize too, that it's the density (compactness) of that sinking section that dictates sink rate—not overall weight.

You are probably wondering what happened to the aforementioned KISS principle. Can we somehow muddle through this myriad mess of confounding information, bringing all this murky business of lengths and weights of line out into the light? Is it possible? It is, indeed, and we're going to deal with that in a moment. First, if you're new at this game, forget all about the vast variety of fly lines out there from which to choose. It's simply mind-boggling. For openers, focus on matching a weight-forward fly line to what the rod manufacturer states. Just focus. Do not buy anything just yet. Next, determine where in the water column you want to be. For example, are you fishing a streamer fly in shallow water? Fine. Consider a two- or three-foot leader attached to a weight-forward 8 floating line, abbreviated as WF-8-F, to match your 8-weight rod. Wish to fish several feet farther down in the water column? Great. Move up the scale to an intermediate sink rate line, a fast sink rate line, or an extra fast sink rate line determined by inches per second. Select a good name brand line such as Airflo, Cortland, Orvis, Scientific Anglers, or Teeny.

Want to add distance as well as get down into the water column where the fish generally are? Fantastic. Assuming that you've had some fly-casting indoctrination as covered in chapter four, and realize that shooting tapers (full sink or speed-sink/floating sinking lines) are executed differently than conventional weight-forward floating lines, let us move up the scale in terms of both line and rod weight to an intermediate Teeny Series T-400 24-foot sinking/58-foot floating section with a sink rate of 8 inches per second. You are now covered quite nicely for bass, blues, weakfish, false albacore, et cetera. Why the Teeny T-400? Three answers, basically. One: because the 10-weight is right in the middle of the recommended rating for rod weights of 8 through 12. Two: because I have worked with the T-300; that is, one down from the T-400—still within the recommended 7- through 10- rod weights; a great line for a *lighter* 8- or 9-weight rod. Three: because I worked with the T-500—one up from the T-400—still within the recommended 9- through 14- rod weights; a great line for a *heavier* 11- or 12-weight rod. Get the picture? Unfortunately, experimentation between rod and line weight is the only way to personify precision. A visit to a professional fly-fishing shop will save you time, money and frustration. These knowledgeable folks will advise and guide you to the right church, right pew. Joining a fly-fishing club, too, where you can ask questions is a good place to start. In our area, Eastern Flyrodders of Long Island (www.easternflyrodders.com) is an excellent group of talented folks. Prior to meetings, during clement weather, club members are afforded the opportunity to receive professional casting instruction—at no charge—from a certified casting instructor.

With regard to shooting tapers, especially for beginners, why purchase Teeny fly lines over another brand? Answer: In part, because Jim Teeny, president of Teeny Incorporated, is the innovator of integrating the floating section to the sinking portion of the line. All one piece. No knots. No splicing. No hinging. To reiterate from the previous chapter, two colors determine its sweet spot; the perfect balancing point. There is no guesswork in determining when to shoot the line. When the second color extends approximately one foot past the rod tip, it's the magic moment. And when it comes to cutting the wind, which is the bane of many a saltwater fly-fisherman, shooting this type of line through a blow is simply a breeze. Pun and fun intended, but it is true. The lines mentioned above retail from $48 to $62. Check Teeny's Web site: www.jimteeny.com. for more information and great videos which cover other fly lines.

Although Teeny carries a wide assortment of fly lines tapers—both single color and the two color system—I'd opt for the two-color system for optimum casting results. Give yourself that added edge whether you are a newcomer or an old salt. I had purchased a couple of Teeny weight-forward 90-foot floating lines under their Supporting Project Healing Waters program: specifically a 5-weight and an 8-weight. The front section (sinking) is blue; the back section (floating) is gold. Those two lines are terrific.

A book on saltwater fly-fishing that I highly recommend is aptly titled *Fly Fishing in Salt Water* by Lefty Kreh. You want the latest edition, published by The Lyons Press ~ $19. 95. It is an invaluable source for the new recruit as well as serving as a great reference book for the veteran.

Leaders & Tippets

Resign yourself to the fact early on that there is no one perfect leader for all saltwater applications. Different types of fly lines will pretty much dictate the length of leader material required. Being that I advocate shooting tapers for the suds, a good rule of thumb is to utilize shorter leaders for heavier, fast-sinking lines, and longer leaders for slow-sinking lines. These leaders may range between 2 to 16 feet in length. Mainly, a middle-of-the-road approach employing a 10-foot leader looped to an intermediate sinking line is the ticket. However, modifications must be made depending on the species of fish you are targeting as well as where in the water column you wish to fish. I could write a lengthy piece on leaders, but then we'd be diverting from the KISS principle. As this is to be a concise presentment, I'll once again direct you to my saltwater bible, where, in detail, you may expand upon these fundamentals: *Fly Fishing in Salt Water* by Lefty Kreh. Tying your own tapered leaders will not only save you a good deal of money, but it will allow you to build a properly balanced leader needed to accommodate a specific situation.

One formula for building a ten-foot leader, inclusive of tippet (the connection between the leader and the fly) may be constructed as follows. Start by purchasing quality spools of 50-, 40-, 30- and 25-pound test monofilament spinning line (limp as opposed to stiff) manufactured by the same company; also, a small spool of 20-pound test fluorocarbon to be used as tippet material. The first five feet of 50-pound test (the butt section) represents fifty percent of the leader's overall length. Employing the 40-, 30-, and 25-pound test monofilament lines, tie together to construct one-foot sections (allowing approximately an extra inch for tying in each section), connecting them with surgeon's knots (simply, a doubled overhand knot). Don't get carried away with precise measurements. Approximations will be fine. Lastly, tie in a two-foot section of 20-pound test fluorocarbon. You will find that this formula will neatly unroll and straighten out leader and tippet, assisting in turning over and properly presenting the fly.

So there you have it, folks. Fly Rods, Reels, Lines, Backing, Leaders and Tippets. With all the time and moola you'll save, you can take your spouse out to dinner and tell her/him some tall tale to rationalize the purchase of all your new toys and ancillary items.

Chapter 6

TOOLS FOR GETTING STARTED IN FLY TYING

This chapter will save you a considerable amount of time and money (not to mention aggravation). We'll begin by selecting the proper tools needed to enjoy this relaxing and rewarding hobby of fly tying. Too, the information will immediately clear away any cobwebs of confusion surrounding an otherwise overwhelming list of products from which to choose, thereby shedding the light of knowledge that will aid you in making informed decisions. In the following chapter, we'll cover the essential materials.

Vises

The first investment you will need to make in getting started in the fascinating world of tying both freshwater and saltwater imitations is a fly-tying vise, and I use the word *investment* judiciously. A fly-tying vise simply holds and locks the hook securely. You do not have to shell out a lot of shekels in order to find a decent vise to do just that. However, a good fly-tying vise does so much more than simply hold a hook securely. Consequently, there are several considerations to explore before purchasing any vise. Personally, I feel that you are going to shortchange yourself in the long-run if you do not at least explore rotary-type vises as opposed to the standard non-rotary style. A visit to your local fly-fishing tackle shop is well worth your time and effort, for within those walls are knowledgeable folks who will be delighted to show you several vises and what they are capable of doing. You are certainly going to spend more money for a true rotary vise, but even if you wind up (pun intended) tying occasionally, I believe you are going to be happier with a rotary style. Why? The short answer is that you will be able to tie virtually any pattern proficiently—proportional to your level of experience, of course—without the frustration you are sure to suffer otherwise.

A basic understanding of hook sizes is paramount in determining what vise will suit your needs. The smallest of hook sizes is a #32 and will progress in largeness to a #1 before receiving a 1/0 designation. From a 1/0, we climb up the scale to a 19/0. I feel it safe to say that most fly tiers, novices to pros, covering a wide spectrum of fly patterns, tie within a range between #22 and 10/0. Tying on either side of that number classification is tying in the extreme. To create an image in your mind, a #32 hook would appear approximately the same size as a question mark on this page. Got the picture? A 19/0 would hang a side of beef, or I should say, so as not to be accused of mixing metaphors, a sizable shark. To further illustrate the point (please excuse another pun), Frank Mundus, of world shark-fishing fame—the inspiration for Captain Quint, the character in Peter Benchley's novel, *Jaws*—used a 10/0 and 12/0 to fight both the 3,427- and 4,500-pound great white sharks (before harpooning the latter). In fact, says Mundus, in an e-mail to me for an article I was writing, "A 19/0 is so big that you can't set the hook past the barb." Therefore, a vise that can accommodate hook sizes from #22 to 10/0 is certainly more than adequate for most fly-tying needs. Is my point well-taken? I thought so.

A well-known name in rotary vises is Renzetti, and sales personnel are sure to point you in that direction. There are several models from which to choose. For example, their Master model accommodates hook sizes from a small freshwater #28 to the much larger 10/0 for serious saltwater applications. Along with that versatility is attached a hefty price tag of $666. But do you, as a beginner, need to spend that kind of money for a true rotary vise in order to tie flies? Absolutely not. Renzetti's new Presentation Model 2000 sells for $300. This vise will handle hook sizes from #28 to 4/0. Therefore, if you wish to tie flies employing larger hooks, you're limited. For the more budget-minded soul, Renzetti sells their Traveler rotary model through Cabela's catalog for $195. But you're still limited because, once again, those vises do not take you beyond the 4/0 barrier. That amounts to, by all accounts, as being penny-wise and pound foolish if you are going to tie large saltwater streamer patterns. If you know that you are going to tie sizable flies and wish to cover a wide range of hook sizes with a true rotary vise that virtually does it all—and for a very fair price—explore the following:

The Dyna-King Supreme is a beefier vise than a Renzetti, and one that will handle a wide range of small and large hook sizes, from #22 on up to 10/0. I strongly suggest that you look into the Dyna-King Supreme. One nice feature that the Supreme model has is that you can adjust the angle of the vise body and its tension by simply adjusting a nut. Too, you have your choice of a clamp-on or the more portable pedestal base for the same dollars, unlike the Renzetti. But for more than a single reason, I opted for the Dyna-King Supreme when I upgraded from my old Renzetti Traveler Model 2003, which still serves me well when tying hook sizes 4/0 and below. The Supreme's rock-solid pedestal with non-skid feet, which weighs 5½ pounds and measures 4 x 5.5 inches, is Gibraltar-like.

The rotary Dyna-King Supreme at $300 is truly a superbly built vise with jaws that remind me of a great white—not in terms of size, of course, but in terms of strength and function. It has all the important features of the Renzetti Master vise, and then some, at less than half the price! Dyna-King's Supreme model features a Notch-Lock cam system that has two curved grooves (pockets): the rear one for easily locking in large saltwater wide-gaped hooks such as 10/0, the forward notch for securing medium sizes, as well as the jaw tip for handling smaller hook sizes down to #22 for freshwater fanatics. If you plan on tying flies down to size #32, midge jaws are available as an option. That is quite an extensive range.

Too, the jaws of the Dyna-King Supreme are superior in design for tying flies on sizable hooks. The vise's hardened tool steel-notched pockets along both facing sides, in addition to forgiving machined serrations that lock in much smaller hooks (in lieu of deeply cut and damaging serrations that bite) are incorporated into the tip, offering a secure hold while significantly limiting the amount of pressure that would ordinarily be required to accomplish the same job. By accommodating and locking in a specific *range* of hook sizes, the force is always applied forward toward the tip. Once a certain size hook is locked into place, it is unnecessary to reposition others that follow, for the Notch-Lock system allows the cam handle to lock in the same position while maintaining the same tension without further adjustment. These features are not found on the more expensive Renzetti Master model. Such smooth facing jaws integrated into the Renzetti models are simply not as conducive to tying truly sizable flies as is the Dyna-King Supreme. It is still another of several reasons why I upgraded to what I believe to be the king of vises over others that sell for more than twice as much. The Dyna-King Supreme is, indeed, just that: supreme. This is one seriously built vise, from body to base, and well worth the money. You can spend upwards of $700 for a rotary vise. That is positively unnecessary. Therefore, I'd strongly suggest the Dyna-King Supreme. Buy it right the first time; buy it once. That's my advice.

If I haven't convinced you at this point to go with a <u>true</u> rotary, then I'll suggest that you look into the HMH Spartan for $199. HMH also has a model called the Standard for $295. There is no need to spend the extra $96 because the HMH Spartan has many of the fine features as its more expensive sibling. For its overall quality, you will not find a finer standard vise for the money than the HMH Spartan. Could you find other standard vises for less money—far less money? Surely, but then you'd be spinning your wheels. Try before you buy is sound advice and should be adhered to regarding the purchase of any vise, especially if you are left handed.

Note: There are vises that may be converted from right- to left-hand operation. With the Dyna-King Supreme, you would simply turn the vise around and put the pivot head lock nut on the other side. Check with your dealer referencing other vises.

Bobbins

A bobbin is a tool that holds a spool of thread and allows you to wind it around the shank of a hook in order to tie in and secure fly-tying materials. The narrow metal tube of the bobbin may or may not be lined with an inner ceramic tube. This fact will determine its cost. Depending on how often you tie should be your gauge in deciding which type of bobbin will suffice. Here is an area where you *could* economize, for it will be a while before the tube of a less expensive bobbin will cause the fine fibers of the thread to chafe, wear, and finally break. So why do that? As we move through this list of fly-tying items, I'll point out where I feel you should and shouldn't try to economize. You could pay close to $30 for a top-notch bobbin with a click-drag adjustment that controls tension, has a longer reaching tube, and is ceramic-lined; or you could spend $3 for a cheaper non-ceramic-lined bobbin. But by leaning toward the middle of those two extremes and selecting a ceramic-lined bobbin for all-around use in the neighborhood of $13, makes the most sense. Why not the cheapest? The answer is because if you are going to be working with materials that require a lot of torque to manipulate, such as flaring, spinning and locking in deer hair, that $3 bargain bobbin might not be the ticket after all.

Bobbins that boast tension control adjustments or ergonomic style is what boosts the price, too. Simply wrapping the thread once or twice around one of the legs of the bobbin will give you all the tension control you'll need; otherwise, your thumb neatly controls the necessary tension in the normal operation of wrapping thread. As a final note in selecting a bobbin, make sure it can accommodate larger spools that contain 200 yards of thread, not just 100 yards.

Bobbin Threaders

Once the spool is on the bobbin, you need to run the thread up and out through the tube of the tool. This is not at all like threading a needle; you have little if any control. A bobbin threader is simply a long, thin-looped wire with a handle that allows you to pass the metal filament down the tube and out so as to feed the thread—much like an oversized eye in a needle; $2 well spent.

Anecdote: In order to save a couple of bucks, I once had the bright idea of using plastic dental floss loops that I picked up at a bargain-basement sale. I inserted the item through the bobbin's tube to catch and pull up the thread. Invariably, those loops would break. I believe I went through an entire package before realizing that this was not as cost effective as I had initially thought. A quick Google search for the brand of dental floss loops I had purchased told me why they broke so easily. They were designed for prison safety. They could not be made into a rope. They could not be used to pick locks and handcuffs. They could not be used as a weapon or a saw. More importantly, those dental floss loops did not substitute as bobbin threaders. There is really little economizing here, folks. Spend the two bucks and get yourself a bobbin threader tool. That's my two-cents worth of advice on bobbin threaders.

Scissors

As important as a rotary vise is to fly tying, a good pair of scissors is just as significant a tool. Generally speaking, you get what you pay for with regard to scissors. My advice is to buy the best pair of scissors that your budget will allow because cutting materials with a pair of cheap scissors just doesn't cut it—both figuratively and literally speaking. Start with a pair of name-brand, all-purpose, straight-bladed, 4½-inch scissors engineered for this purpose. Stainless steel will cost you. Scissors should meet three criteria: the finger holes should be large enough to accommodate your digits comfortably; the scissors must have fine points for fine work; they must be sharp. Good fly-tying scissors have serrated edges that you can barely see. They are machined as such. A pair of dull scissors will shift the material rather than cut smoothly as the blades are meshed together.

Additionally, if you find yourself working with deer hair and creating heads and bodies on flies that need to be shaped, you will soon discover that a pair of curved scissors will make the job considerably easier and neater. However, you can hold off on this purchase until the time arises, utilizing the all-purpose type in the meantime. The important thing to keep in mind when using your scissors is to employ the tips of the blades when cutting fine threads and materials. When cutting coarser material, use the back section of the blades. Tungsten-carbide or titanium scissors are especially strong, so I have a second pair on hand for cutting and trimming tougher materials. If you have kids, regardless of their ages, hide those scissors. They are not to be used on anything but hairs, fibers, fur, flash, feathers and thread. If *you* use them to cut lead wire and such, you will dull them in a heartbeat; consequently, your expensive tools should be taken away from you as immediate punishment. The price range of a pair of good to great fly-tying scissors will run $15 to $70 depending on the elements covered above. Again, I'd advise you to buy the best that your budget will permit—perhaps starting somewhere in the middle of that spread. At the top end, a pair of Ice 4½-inch tempered stainless steel scissors manufactured by F. W. Engels of Solingen, Germany, will cost approximately $70. Dr. Slick is another brand name I'd explore toward the other end of the pricing spectrum.

Bodkins or Dubbing Needles

A bodkin or dubbing needle is nothing more than approximately a one-inch needle in a 2-inch handle. You could fashion one out of a dowel and, yes, a sewing needle or pin. It is used primarily to apply a droplet of head cement to thread wraps in order to secure them. Also, it is used to pick at before cutting unwanted fibers, or to tease such fibers in order to create a desired effect. Too, it may be used to assist in tying a series of half hitches so as to secure a wrap. It is, indeed, a handy little tool; but I wouldn't pay more than a few bucks. They have fancier ones on the market to justify your spending more money. Don't get reeled in. A bobbin threader and a bodkin are about as inexpensive as it's going to get, guys and gals. Make or buy a bodkin for no more than $3.

Hackle Pliers

Hackle pliers allow you the dexterity to neatly wrap materials around the shank of a hook; for example, yarn, chenille, floss and tinsel for ribbing—or feathers so as to form leggy bodies and collars. Admittedly, this can be done by hand, but not with the control and tension needed to securely place those wraps *precisely* where you want them. There are a good many hackle pliers on the market, but not a one I found that met my requirements wrapped up in a single package. It's not a perfect world but not the end of the world either. Most importantly, the jaws of the tool must be able to maintain enough tension necessary to hold a hackle (feather) firmly in place while winding without it slipping. Look for a pair of non-skid hackle pliers that incorporate a serrated grip on one end of the tip and a rubber sleeve-covering on the other. I have a decent pair made by Tiemco. If you can locate strong hackle pliers with two rubber or silicone tips—in lieu of the one serrated metal tip/one rubber—so much the better. Next, it would be nice if all hackle pliers had a large enough ring-opening in its handle to accommodate your finger so as to rotate the tool freely. Again, Tiemco has one with a nice, large silicone ring in its handle; however, the tool's weight is too light. Ideally, those pliers should be heavy enough to hold the hackle firmly in place for a hands-free operation while you're performing another function. What to do? Wingaersheek Flies, online at www.wflies.com, sells a heavier, large-sized set of English style hackle pliers made by Seaport. They are stronger and heavier than the Tiemco pair and have adequate room for finger rotation. What they do not have, however, is a protective rubber or silicone sleeve at the tip. What I did was to improvise, removing the rubber tip from the Tiemco set and slipping it onto the Seaport pair. Good to go. I still use the Tiemco pliers for very light duty. I'm sure that if I searched, I could locate and cut a tiny piece of narrow rubber tubing to affix to those tips. Approximately $10 covered the cost of both pair.

Whip Finishers

There is only one whip finisher on the market that I would recommend. It is the Matarelli whip finishing tool. This implement allows you to place thread wraps exactly where you want them. Actually, I have two: the Matarelli Standard model, and the Matarelli Long-Reach model. Your other alternative is your fingers. Lefty Kreh, world renowned fly-caster/fly-tier/author, would insist that you learn how to whip finish the head of a fly by hand. Too, once you learn the method, it's a relatively simple process to extend the reach into other areas of the fly that would otherwise be inaccessible with the standard Matarelli tool, thereby eliminating the need for either Matarelli device. So then why am I encouraging you to go out and purchase the Matarelli Standard tool? Again, this implement allows you to place those thread wraps *exactly* where you want them. You may not be able to accomplish this even after considerable practice in whip finishing a fly by hand. I most definitely encourage you to learn how to whip finish by using your fingers. Still, there are times you will wish you had that tool. The Standard model retails for $16; the Long Reach is $20.

Tweezers, Beadzers (reverse tweezers) & Nail Clippers

There are several shapes and sizes to tweezers and beadzers that serve a variety of fly tying functions. They are handy for picking up tiny items such as beads, dumbbell eyes, hooks and other such items that we store in compartmentalized plastic boxes. It is not at all necessary to shop for these two tools in fly-fishing tackle shops or through related catalogs. The corner drugstore, supermarket or variety store is your best bet. While you're there, pick up a set of both small and large nail clippers for cutting such items as monofilament line (used for 'glass' bodied minnows), making weed guards, et cetera. You're looking at approximately $15 for tweezers, beadzers and the two nail clippers. I wouldn't go out of my way if you can't locate beadzers right away; tweezers will serve in a pinch. Am I not a punster?

Threads

Yes, your thread may be considered a tool, too. The number of manufactures, sizes and colors from which to choose can be overwhelming, but we'll immediately narrow the list in order to get you started. Actually, one company, one size and five colors fill most of my own fly-tying needs for saltwater applications.

For salt water, a 200-yard spool of Danville's Flat-Waxed Nylon for around $4 is an excellent all-purpose thread that you can really torque down without fear of it breaking. The beauty of this thread is that it can be worked flat, or it can be slightly twisted so as to pinch down when flaring and spinning deer hair, thereby eliminating the need to purchase other threads to accomplish the same job. For example, some shops may suggest spools of size "A", lightly waxed and round-twisted Danville's FlyMaster Plus for specifically flaring and spinning deer hair (which come in 100-yard spools for $2. However, many fly tiers do not realize that Danville's Flat-Waxed Nylon does double duty, thereby eliminating the need to purchase FlyMaster Plus. As a matter of fact, the two threads are approximately the same diameter. Do the math; you have just saved four bucks.

As you won't initially be going up or down in size using Danville's Flat-Waxed Nylon (designated as 210-Denier), I suggest ordering several colors that will carry you along quite nicely: olive, white, red, black, yellow. Simply as a point of information, and in order to shed some light on the confusing world of thread and their diameter designations, the Denier System is a unit of weight equal to one gram per every 9000 meters of fiber. This is quite a different system from the standard lettering and numbering method that will be explained momentarily.

For freshwater applications, I'd suggest going down in diameter, but not too far down to where you might tend to break the thread on your first attempt at tying. For starting out tying freshwater flies, a 3/0 diameter is the ticket. I recommend purchasing a 100-yard spool of white Danville's 3/0 Pre-Waxed Monocord; a flat monofilament thread with a fine finish for $1.75. As you progress, you will graduate to a finer 4/0 diameter thread, then on to a 5/0 or 6/0, and so forth. Therefore, do not stock up on these spools of thread in smaller diameters and varying colors just yet. Stick with this spool of white 3/0 and go from there. As you become more experienced, you may want to familiarize yourself with threads from other manufacturers such as Gudebrod, Griffith, and Uni (a small Canadian company). Stay away from Kevlar thread. Although it has undeniable strength, it will, in time, play havoc with your bobbin and scissors.

Referencing thread sizes, let's take a quick look at what the *standard* numbering system actually means. A 3/0 diameter thread is thicker and therefore stronger than a 6/0, the latter of which is a finer diameter thread generally used for smaller flies tied on smaller hooks. 6/0 is an abbreviated form of (six zeros) 6/000000. The more zeros, the finer the thread. The number 6 preceding the six zeros is abridged to 6/0 for the practicality of manufacturer labeling. Once down to a single 0, specified as 1/0, the labeling system shifts to the letters "A", "B", "C" and so forth. Seldom will you see larger than an "A" thread diameter used in fly tying. "B", "C", "D" and up-the-alphabet of thread diameters would be used in rod building. The further along the alphabet, the greater the diameter. The greater the number of zeros, the finer the diameter. For comparison's sake, a Danville's Flat-Waxed Nylon (210-Denier—a system of measurement unto itself) is the equivalent of an "A" designation, that is, thicker in diameter and consequently stronger than a 1/0, but not as thick or as strong as a "B". And please do not embroil yourself in inane arguments when they arise regarding the breaking strength of working flat thread versus twisted, or the contention that waxed fiber may have some bearing on these approximations, for they are just that: close estimates. Some folks love to complicate matters; others simply want to have fun. Let's put ourselves in the latter category.

Tool Caddy

For me, organization is the key to keeping one's sanity intact while coursing through our busy lives. There is going to come a point, and rather quickly, when you will need something in which to store all those items that you will most assuredly accumulate for fly tying. One such article is Renzetti's non-slip, soft foam tool caddy. It is simply the perfect organizer; it has no equal. Thirty-five round compartments (from ¼- to 1¼-inch diameters) and two square sections (1½ x 1½ inches) allow you to hold virtually any fly-tying tool, along with ancillary items such as glues, epoxies, head cement, et cetera. Should the foam become exposed to these agents, resulting from a spill, Renzetti claims their caddy is impervious to these chemicals. I couldn't tell you for sure, thank goodness. What I find very handy, too, are 35mm film canisters in which to hold toothpicks, thicker applicator sticks, as well as various and sundry paraphernalia. For easy access, the film containers fit neatly into four of the aforementioned compartments. To have everything readily available and highly visible on the table is a godsend. The cost of this fine, foam block—measuring 8 x 5 x 2 inches—is $20.

Lighting

If you cannot see clearly without straining your eyes, you are not going to enjoy this marvelous hobby. Therefore, proper lighting is of paramount importance. Daylight is your best source of illumination. Therefore, try and find a window offering the most available natural light. Set up your work area accordingly. Of course, there are going to be times when you will have to depend on artificial light. Finding the proper light that is most conducive to fly tying can be tricky. In searching for such an item, you might find yourself in the dark, for there are a battery of bulbs from which to choose—lamps that boast bright halogen beams, fluorescent tube types, LEDs with magnifiers, incandescent, luminescent, and daylight-simulation illumination.

You want the latter, that is, a lamp with a low-heat bulb that simulates daylight. You do not want a blinding bright light that is going to create glare. You want Ott-Lite technology. You want to view true color as you would during daylight hours. Ott-Lite technology is a high definition natural daylight lighting system that offers the ultimate for hobbyists who need near-perfect lighting conditions. I have portable power at my fingertips with an adjustable 11- to 19-inch flip-lid Ott-Lite as well as their gooseneck-type lamps. They are ideal for detail work. It is the closest lighting you will find next to true daylight. If the Greek cynic Diogenes were alive today, he would be combing the streets of Athens during midday with an Ott-Lite in lieu of his lantern—in search of an honest man. I will honestly tell you that you'll love your Ott-Lite. Its inventor, Dr. (Ph. D.) John Ott, the father of full spectrum light, has shed some serious illumination on this subject. At a price range from $50 to $90, you cannot go wrong.

So there you have it. Further fatherly advice is to stay far away from fly-fishing tool kits that also feature a standard non-rotary vise—all for the remarkable price of $25 to $40! Well, you'll get what you pay for: inferior merchandise by comparison to the fine tools we just covered. Running through this list and averaging the costs of the items mentioned, I come up with $450 to $550, depending on which vise you select—plus Uncle Sammy's cut; namely, tax. Not a bad deal to get started in a hobby that could carry you through a lifetime of fun, relaxation, and great satisfaction. I have created and elaborated on fly patterns that have proved quite successful. Your success will only be limited by your imagination as you progress. I have included my fly recipes along with other proven patterns in a subsequent chapter; but first things first.

Chapter 7

MATERIALS FOR GETTING STARTED IN FLY TYING

If one is not careful, one could easily wind up with enough feathers, furs, fibers and flash material to fill several king-size pillowcases. This caveat does not only apply to the beginner; it certainly addresses the accomplished flytier as well. Falling somewhere between those two poles, I could easily fill two king-size pillowcases. This is not hyperbole, nor did the accumulation of material happen overnight. It happened gradually. It happened imperceptibly over the course of many years, beginning with tying freshwater streamers, nymphs, emergers and dry flies for trout, bluegills, large and smallmouth bass, perch, pickerel and pike—continuing with saltwater patterns such as Lefty's Deceivers and Bob Clouser's Minnows for bluefish, striped bass and weakfish.

In getting started in fly tying, we will concentrate on the basics, covering fundamental materials crowning a wide range of patterns that will certainly catch fish from Maine to Florida, as well as beyond those boundaries. If I had said "around the world," you might quietly accuse me of gross exaggeration. Therefore, I'll tread cautiously and alert you to the fact that the materials we shall explore together are used globally. You will need less than two dozen materials in order to get started properly. Those items can easily be stored in a desk drawer, a designated box, or displayed (not strewn) along your tying table for easy accessibility.

Hackles: (saddles, capes, skins—confusion)

Generally speaking, **hackles** refer to the feathers of birds. Referencing fly tying, **saddle hackles** are commonly referred to those feathers found below the neck of the bird, specifically—but not categorically—the posterior (back) section. The term saddle hackle oftentimes leads to confusion as it can refer to the softer feathers found along and below the neck on the hen (female fowl) as opposed to the stiffer feathers found on the rooster (male fowl). More frequently, however, the term saddle hackle is used interchangeably referencing both sexes. To add to the confusion when employing the word hackle by itself—used in its noun form—some will argue that the feather only applies to that of the rooster. To hackle the body of a fly—used as a verb—simply means to palmer (wrap) a feather around the artificial. In this sense, hackle applies to either gender. To keep it simple, hen hackle is largely employed in tying wet flies, that is, flies that will readily sink below the surface simply because the softer feather absorbs water. Rooster feathers, conversely, are commonly used in tying dry flies because they resist absorption, trap air bubbles, and therefore aid in keeping the fly afloat. Chiefly, hackle feathers come from both the male and female gender of our common domestic chicken. Other feathers come from waterfowl, primarily ducks, as well as upland game birds such as grouse, pheasant, quail, partridge, et cetera. Whereas saddle hackle can refer to the area below the base of the neck of both hen and cock, a **cape** is commonly called a rooster neck. A **skin** from either sex includes the top of the bird's head, its neck, flank (shoulders–wings), saddle and tail; in other words, the whole feathery bird. As a rule of thumb when tying wet flies, soft saddle hackles from the hen are tied in by their tips. When tying dry flies, the stiffer cape (neck) hackles from the rooster are tied in by their quills. You now have a fairly good handle on saddles, capes and skins.

Please keep the following in mind in order to keep your sanity. As a rule, saddle hackles (as compared to cape hackle) possess stems that are thinner, exhibit more curvature, display broader, rounder tips, and are webby. Capes possess stiffer stems, exhibit less curvature, display pointy tips, and are less webby. I trust that this elaboration helps clear away the cobwebs.

Selecting saddles & capes

As most fish are taken on wet flies, let's explore hen and rooster hackles worth their weight a hundred-fold. Colors can and do vary widely. First off, if I had but two colors to choose in getting started, I'd select dun-colored hackles (a brownish-gray) along with white. You will hear the phrase "match the hatch," referring to replicating the emergence of nymphs, aquatic insects and minnows in freshwater applications. It is also applied to saltwater situations when imitating bigger baitfish. You can generally purchase these hackles in quarter or half saddles as well as full skins. I advise that you buy what your budget will allow but suggest considering a complete skin from both a hen and rooster. You will then have on hand the proper sized feathers covering a wide range of tying needs. For example, you can now coordinate opposing curved feathers from each side of a saddle or cape for creating wings and tails on streamers and such. If you can cover the cost of complete skins, consider these four colors: dun, white, black, and brown—or combinations thereof, referred to as grizzly, badger, ginger, et cetera. Generally speaking, bright, showy colors catch fishermen, not necessarily fish. Dull colors will make your day. Another advantage to purchasing these full skins is that you will have a nice assortment for covering a wider range of hook sizes with which to work. Explore the wonderful world of feather hunting by logging on to both Whiting Farms' and Metz Feathers' Web sites. Note, too, that you can buy by the grade, such as a quality #1 or #2—generally meaning the number of feathers as opposed to their quality per se. Again, let your budget be your guide.

Peacock Herl

Peacock herl is a greenish-blue iridescent material from—you guessed it—the peacock; the male of the peafowl family. The material may be purchased in craft stores, as it is used for decorative purposes. Its fronds can be found strung along a base of cord in packaging, bundled loosely, or purchased as a full tail. The quills are, indeed, delicate; however, there are tricks of the trade to make the material bulletproof. As an attractor, it may be found wound around bodies for a segmented effect, forming collars, or displayed in lengths as toppings for wet flies, especially streamers. It is absolutely deadly. Freshwater trout especially fall prey to this devastating magnetic-like hue, but don't underestimate its ability to attract pelagic species as well.

Yarn

Yarn can and should be purchased in a fabric store rather than buying single or assorted packages of the material in a fly-tying shop. If you commit such folly, you are paying for that merchandising several times over. Better yet, a spouse's or neighbor's crocheting or knitting basket is sure to yield a handful of assorted colors and shades thereof. That is all you really need to get started. Thick pieces of yarn can be pulled apart to form thinner strands, or altered to create dubbing material. You're in business.

Chenille

Chenille is a yarn with a protruding pile. You can also purchase this item in fabric stores just as you may obtain many other articles germane to fly tying. Look around or ask a salesperson for small packaged or miniature card-wrapped quantities of chenille as opposed to buying a single skein. Search for yellows, pinks, olives, and reds.

Floss

Floss is a glossy, absorbent threadlike material used mainly to build up bodies or create decorative bands along the hook shank. Therefore, it is well-suited in tying wet flies. Today, most floss material is made from strands of rayon, whereas years ago, shiny silk floss was traditionally used to tie salmon flies. Select a spool of four-strand floss that usually comes in ten-yard lengths. Let's run with red for starters.

Deer Hair

Deer hair obtained from the animal's hide, including its tail (bucktail), are essential fly-tying materials. Don't leave the fly-tackle shop without them, for you won't find any in craft stores. The items come in their natural gray/brown and white shades as well as an assortment of dyed colors covering any chromatic hue imaginable. Select one natural swatch-sized section from the belly and one bucktail from the North American white-tailed deer. Choose a natural gray/brown and white medium tone as opposed to a darker shade. Also, select one soft yellow bucktail, one pink, and one black. We will be using these colors in a particular fly-tying recipe. Later, we'll be working with several colors. But for now, we'll start with the basics. The important thing is in knowing what the hair from the belly and tail (two extremes in performance) entails in tying—and why. In selecting bucktail, pick the biggest, softest tails you can find. The top of the tail, that is, nearest the tip, is marvelous for tying saltwater streamer flies. The hair at the base of the tail tends to flair as you tie it in tightly; nevertheless, it has definite advantages and is not to be discarded.

Hair taken from the belly of the deer flares and/or spins dramatically when torque is applied by the thread. This is exactly what you want it to do. It is a fantastic material for building bodies and heads on flies of all sizes. Packing in and torquing down bunch after bunch upon the shank of the hook allows you to actually sculpt flared and/or spun deer hair. Although this coarse hair from the belly section of the body is not actually hollow, in the sense that a straw is hollow, its cellular structure, which allows the hair to flare, does indeed trap air and aid in keeping the fly afloat. However, if you wish for that fancy piece of artwork to sink below the surface, wrapping wire around the hook shank (beforehand) for added weight is the ticket so as to get that fly down into the water column. This leads us to the next useful and necessary material.

Wire

You can buy lead wire (some frown on its use) in a fly-tying shop, or you can head toward your local hardware store and pick up a small roll of .020 fuse wire. As mentioned earlier, most fish are taken below the surface. You can either wrap the wire directly around the hook shank, or first build up a base of thread in order to help support lengths of wire beneath, atop, or alongside the shank so as to control what you wish that fly to do down in the water column. For example; you could have the hook ride upside down, creating some deadly flies tied Clouser style—named after Bob Clouser, veteran flytier—or you might give it a crippled effect by having it ride to one side. You can even create a kind of keel with 'matchbook' lead strips to help keep the fly tracking true.

Tinsel and Flash

Tinsel and flash materials are shiny attractors. Tinsel is a thin, narrow metal strip used to wrap the hook shank or body of the fly. Try a spool of 1/16-inch copper color as opposed to the usual choices of gold and/or silver. Flash material, made of Mylar, comes in a myriad of mind-boggling colors and is packaged in long, thin, film-like narrow strips—sold under a number of labels such as Flashabou and Krystal Flash. It is a fantastic material for streamer flies. If I had but one *color* selection to choose from, it would be rainbow flash. This might sound like the proverbial genie in the bottle granting a single wish, to which I would wisely reply, "My one wish is for you to grant me several other wishes." Rainbow flash is a killer. The key to tying in most materials is to tie sparsely. You are striving to create a profile, not build a brush with which to paint the side of a barn in a single stroke. When you graduate to tying flies with schlappen (large feathers), especially used for shark fishing, that's another story . . . and will be when I hook into one worthy of mention. Pick up a package of red flash material, too. You will need it to simulate gills.

Eyes

Eyes are an important anatomy of the fly. You will catch fish without imitating them. You will catch *more* fish by adding that part of their anatomy to your pattern. Whether you paint on peepers, burn in a pair, figure-eight dumbbell or bead chain balls onto the hook shank with thread, epoxy over prism-tape orbs, or glue-gun large molded 3-D-like lamps—the eyes have it! The eyes are your window of opportunity to score big. I have eyes in every medium mentioned above and then some. I have eyes in many sizes and colors. Allow me to share with you what works well: a black pupil with a golden rim, that is, the iris. In keeping things simple for starters, I'll suggest flat, prism tape stick-on eyes. These eyes are fabricated from a multi-layered mix of pearlescent and clear Mylar, thereby reflecting light much like that of a fish's iris, which is found to be flat in most cases. The eyes of baitfish are the predators' targets.

I ask that you hunt up pairs of flat, prism tape, paste-on, golden-rimmed eyes with black pupils that we will need later for our fly-tying recipe. These sizes are measured in inches or millimeters. Look for small 2.5mm eyes that are equal to 5/32-inch. Also, larger 6mm eyes corresponding to 11/32-inch. These are overall dimensions encompassing the iris and the pupil. Try coming as close as you can to these measurements. If you have trouble locating exact sizes, not to worry because we will have some wiggle room. The eyes usually come fixed to small, narrow cards. They are fairly inexpensive; therefore, if you can go one size up and down on either side of the scale, so much the better. You will then have a fairly decent range of deadly eyes to start you off. Not to complicate matters, but only to give you some idea when computing the sizes of eyes for fly tying (don't even bother to do the math conventionally), take a peek at the standard conversion table below.

As a reference, the eyes are sized in millimeters from 1.5mm to 12mm. The conversion to inches is as follows. 1.5mm = 3/32; 2.0mm = 1/8; 2.5mm = 5/32; 3mm = 3/16; 3.5mm = 7/32; 4mm = 1/4; 4.5mm = 9/32; 5mm = 5/16; 6mm = 11/32; 6.5mm = 3/8; 7mm = 7/16; 8mm = 1/2; 10mm = 5/8; 12mm = 3/4.

Lady Amherst Pheasant Feathers [Neck, Saddle or Full Skin]

This bird is native to China, but it had been introduced to England; namely, Bedfordshire. Whereas the overall length of the bird is approximately forty inches, in fly-fishing shops it is generally found packaged from the top of its head to the base of its neck; that is, minus its saddle and tail. For approximately a 7- to 8-inch neck (head usually included), you will pay in the neighborhood of $10. It will include the white/black-rimmed tippet feathers of various sizes, behind which are attached much smaller but invaluable dun-colored gimp feathers. We will be using the bird's tippet and gimp feathers for both freshwater and saltwater fly recipes. We'll also work with the metallic green plumage found on the saddle section (back) for an additional pattern. Therefore, if your budget allows, I suggest purchasing a full skin of the Lady Amherst pheasant so that you will have on hand a versatile assortment of feathers with which to cover both freshwater and saltwater applications. Also, you will have a wide range of sizes from which to choose in order to properly accommodate hook/hackle proportion. You will save money in the long run. In a dusty corner of an upstate New York tackle shop, I found a Rumpf & Son, Lady Amherst pheasant skin (no tail), #1 quality, for $10. As mentioned, I usually pay $9 or $10 for just a neck and head. Of course, the likelihood of finding what you're searching for may not be there; however, you might discover another gem. Seek and you shall find bargains.

Marabou Feathers

True marabou feathers come from the marabou stork, which is native to South Africa and the Sahara Desert. These birds are rare. Therefore, as a substitute, our so-called marabou feathers are obtained right here in the United States from under the wing of the domestic white turkey. The Chinese buy them from us by the carload, selecting the largest feathers in order to manufacture boas. For fly-tying purposes, we employ the shorter soft plumes—dyed and available in many different colors and shades thereof. It is an excellent fly-tying material because the downy fluff presents a fluid, lifelike leggy action that is unparalleled. Simply breathing upon a plume immediately lets you know how it is going to behave in the water column when allowed to settle back down after being stripped forward. Its wispy, undulating, underwater movement is a killer and a favorite for tying in wings, tails, legs, collars, et cetera. Generally packaged and labeled as 'strung marabou blood quill,' select a solid white for underbodies, red to simulate gill plates, black for general night fishing, chartreuse and yellow to drive fish mad during daylight hours. I find yellow to be an underrated color whether I'm fishing plugs, tins or flies.

Sometimes you will see packages labeled as Grizzly Marabou. These are soft feathers with natural barred markings found on some chickens, which may be sold under the name Grizzly Chicabou. Stick with turkey marabou for lifelike breathable action. Wapsi is a U.S. company dealing in fly-tying materials whose founder many years ago discovered that the plumes from the turkey are similar to those found on the genuine marabou stork of northern and southern Africa.

Later, after you navigate your way around, you will undoubtedly start to collect other feathers from ducks, geese, partridge, grouse, ostrich, quail, et cetera; hair from moose, elk and other deer as well; fur from mink, fox, rabbit, seal, raccoon —ad infinitum. You won't be able to help yourself.

Fur

A versatile material that we will be using in one of our fly-tying recipes is grizzly (grayish white) crosscut rabbit fur, which is packaged by Orvis in 3-foot by 1/8-inch strips. Be sure to select the crosscut material as opposed to zonker strips, which are uniformly cut lengthwise instead of crosswise. This is but still another deadly material that belongs in your arsenal of fly-tying accoutrements.

Hooks

For our initial saltwater fly tying recipes, pick up a small package of Mustad-O'Shaughnessy style #3407 ~ 1/0 stainless steel hooks, and a small package of Owner hooks, size 2/0 black, short-shank, turned-up eye. For our initial freshwater fly tying recipes, pick up a box of Mustad-Viking #94838, #8 hooks, turned-down eye. This will get you started in covering both freshwater and saltwater applications. Never ever sell yourself short by buying bargain (cheap) hooks.

Epoxy & Head Cements

I have good success with Z-Poxy—a two-part (resin and hardener) five-minute formula—for covering those flat, prism-tape orbs mentioned earlier. Less expensive epoxies that I've used tend to yellow with time. A one-fluid-ounce bottle of Flex-Seal, and a bottle of clear Sally Hanson Hard As Nails-With Nylon (comes with brush) are all you really need to coat, protect, and give a glossy finish to those thread wraps.

In short order, you will have the basic materials to start a most enjoyable hobby. I'd like to repeat the names of the first two companies that produce superior product in reference to the hackles covered herein. I might be accused of feathering their nests, but so be it. You are dealing with quality, period: Whiting Farms and Metz Feathers. There are other good companies out there, but if you begin with the big boys, you won't be disappointed. In the following chapter, we will tie deadly fly patterns for both freshwater and saltwater that will take fish from the northern corner of Canada, down along the coast to the Keys—as well as the inland waters of the northeast.

Chapter 8

FLY TYING FOR BEGINNERS

Many of you have probably already purchased your tools and materials and are raring to go. Others may be well ahead of the game because you couldn't wait to begin, having already received some outside instruction. I can't blame you for that. Impatience is a disease, and fly tying is definitely habit-forming. But I'm going to ask that you carefully read through these initial paragraphs before beginning the fly-tying recipes that follow. I'll even say please because I don't want you to miss out on a step that will more than likely save you some grief, along with incalculable wasted hours. I say this with confidence simply because bad habits become set in stone and not easily broken nor even noticed by others as fly tying is generally a solitary activity. In most situations, no one is standing over you to point out that you are performing a certain procedure incorrectly. In my own case, over the course of several years, I was not even aware that I was performing an important step rather poorly—time and time again.

Let's begin by locking in a standard saltwater Mustad-O'Shaughnessy style #3407 ~ 1/0 stainless steel hook covered in the preceding chapter under Materials. Next, we will load the bobbin with Danville's (210 denier) Flat-Waxed Nylon and simply tie in the thread onto the hook shank. If you feel that you truly have this first step down pat because you couldn't wait and received tutelage elsewhere, you may— but only with written permission—skip this and the next paragraph, but please do not skip the section titled PINCH-WRAPPING for PRACTICE. That said, pull two or three inches of thread from the bobbin as the strand is easier to control than if you were to work with a longer length. Hold the bobbin in one hand; with the other hand, pinch the end of the thread between your thumb and forefinger and position the strand ¼ inch behind the eye of the hook. With light tension, wind the thread clockwise (away from you), over itself and around the hook shank in the direction of the bend. Make a few more contiguous (adjoining) wraps. Let go of the bobbin and let it hang there for a moment. Are your wraps neat? Pull down gently on the bobbin. Is the thread locked in and secure? Cut the loose end. Continue wrapping toward the bend of the hook. Practice making all your wraps abutting one another up to where the thread is perpendicular (vertical) to the point of the hook. Note that in order to continue wrapping all the way up to the very beginning of the bend, you will either have to shorten the length of the thread by retracting it back onto the spool (which is silly), or simply learn to lean the bobbin slightly to the right [if right handed] while wrapping so as to avoid catching and tearing fibers of the thread. Covering this section of the hook with the waxed thread makes a good base on which to tie in feathers, yarn and other such material.

Apart from properly teaching the beginner the first step of tying in thread upon the shank of the hook, I have seen many a veteran fly-tying instructor miss the mark when it came to demonstrating how to secure and lock in materials of denser diameters such as yarn, hackle, or clumps of deer hair. This important instruction was either inadequately explained or the instructor merely failed to mention the operation at all—although pantomimically performing the step correctly. In evaluating this oversight, perhaps the instructor assumed that the process of tying in heavier materials is rote because virtually every adult person on the planet knows how to wrap twine around boxes, ribbons around presents, and a garden hose onto a caddy. Therefore, it should follow that the student innately knows how to wrap and secure these materials around a wire hook. Not so. So let's examine this next all-important step referred to as the pinch-wrap, for it is without a doubt an invaluable function. It would prove prudent to practice the pinch-wrap with a piece of yarn or chenille before playing around with bunches of deer hair or the like.

Pinch-Wrapping For Practice

Let's begin with a 2-inch piece of chenille for practice. Assuming that you are right-handed, a pinch-wrap begins when you employ the thumb and forefinger of your *left* hand to hold the material precisely where you want it before securing it in place—much like when we held the thread between our fingers in the previous operation. However, rather than simply wrapping the thread around the item, the flytier first makes a small, loose wrap over and around the material, catching the thread between the *pinch*, creating tension before slowly torquing down upon the chenille, then over and back around again, each time catching the thread between thumb and forefinger so as to lock the material solidly in place atop the hook. This will prevent the material from sliding off to the side. I can assure you that as you graduate from thicker fibers to flaring and spinning bunches of deer hair, this procedure will prove priceless. Practice this pinch-wrap with materials such as chenille, two-ply yarn, four-ply yarn, flash material, feathers, and finally deer hair, affixing them to the top of the hook shank. The amount of pressure required for the pinch-wrap, weighed against the tension needed to torque down and secure those materials atop the shank, will become second nature to you with a bit of practice. It is this dexterity that is required in order to manipulate those materials without having them travel helter-skelter around the shank of the hook.

Whip Finishing For Practice (using a tool; using your hand)

Place a hook in your visc, then following the directions included with your Matarelli whip-finishing tool, build up a head of thread directly behind the eye of the hook. This procedure is frustrating to many people, not because the directions are poor, but because some folks become too impatient. Impatience is a disease that impairs the mind. For years I tied in a series of half hitches employing a bodkin (dubbing needle) before learning to finish off the head of a fly by hand. Dan Eng of

Eastern Flyrodders of Long Island, a consummate flytier, fly-caster and fly-fisherman, worked with me until I finally caught on. It is important to learn how to whip finish a fly by hand as well as with your Matarelli tool. Read, study and follow those diagrams, step by step, most carefully, until you get it. No ifs, ands or buts. Now, practice, practice, practice.

It is difficult to verbally explain how to finish off a fly by hand without simultaneously demonstrating the procedure visually. Therefore, I recommend the following. Once you have mastered your Matarelli tool, study the principle employed in forming the triangle illustrated in the directions and make the transition of that operation by using your fingers in lieu of the instrument. If you are still having trouble, pick up a video such as Bob Clouser & Lefty Kreh's, Volume 1: *Masters of Fly Tying—Tying Techniques*. The two gentlemen each have some sixty-plus years behind the vise. Lefty both explains and illustrates the manual procedure clearly and concisely. Their collective knowledge in constructing flies is invaluable.

Playing With Epoxy

Mix equal but small amounts of two-part, five-minute epoxy—about the size of half a pencil's eraser. A little bit goes a long way. Using your dubbing needle, apply a dot of this mixture to a built-up head of thread in your vise. A single drop (way too much) will seem like a reservoir. Watch it. Study it. See it sag? Control it by rotating the fly in the vise. The epoxy will set up in approximately five minutes. I generally wait twenty-four hours before applying a light coat of Flex-Seal or a clear nail polish for a glossy finished look. A one-fluid-ounce bottle of Flex-Seal, and a bottle of clear Sally Hanson Hard As Nails-With Nylon are all you need to coat, protect, and give a glossy finish to those thread wraps.

Assuming that you have practiced and mastered these skills, you are about ready to tie your first fly from the recipe presented in the next chapter. As promised, the patterns presented will take fish anywhere in our region and beyond—and they certainly have.

Chapter 9

FLY RECIPES FOR SALT & FRESH WATER

Bob B's Black & White Big Bull's-Eye Fly

Every once in a while a fly design comes along that is quite unique. This black and white, big-eyed, small-fry fly is one such revelation. Why? The short answer is that this Black & White Big Bull's-Eye Fly is especially effective for the reason that its eyes are the very center of consideration and commands the predator's full attention. The long answer is because the **eye of the fly** is, overwhelmingly, the assailant's target, or at least a reference point in terms of attack, whether the strike comes from below and behind, such as bluefish chopping their way through a cloud of peanut bunker, or from a frontal assault, as a striper aiming for the head of a baitfish, annihilating it by inhaling it whole. The dark central opening of the imitation's iris, its pupil, is the attacker's bull's-eye. The fly's oversized eyes, in relationship to its body, are positioned midpoint within the gap of the hook—seemingly gaping at its terminator in a defiant *Dart toward me if you dare!* stare. Succinctly stated, in essence, **the eye *is* the fly**. The eyes will not interfere with the gap of the hook. Upon a strike, those filmy, feathery eyes will collapse or be brushed to one side.

It is a simple fly to tie—so simple that it is tied in four easy steps. Only a particle of patience may be required to secure those big feathered eyes within the gap of the hook your first time out. The fly we are about to tie together is quite effective. The black and white pattern I chose is generic, covering various conditions; for example, bright days, cloudy days, day or night. It is an all-purpose fly meant to target fish rather than fishermen. The imitation can also be tied in a multitude of colors. As far as the colors of the eyes are concerned, I favor a golden iris with a black pupil. The irises of the majority of fish are flat; therefore, I selected prism tape eyes for this particular fly rather than a three-dimensional flare. These eyes are fabricated from a multi-layered mix of pearlescent and clear Mylar, reflecting light very much like that of a fish's iris. With just a touch of epoxy added to the back of the eyes, they adhere faithfully to the feather. Contrarily, 3-D plastic eyes placed within the hook's gap would definitely interfere with a strike. The flat prism tape Mylar eyes simply will not impede a hookup.

A short-shank 2/0 Owner's hook, in black, best serves this big-eyed recipe. This is a black and white fly and, therefore, needs not exhibit the reflective properties of a shiny, encircling stainless steel arc. Only the light mirroring off a pair of prismatic-tape eyes will do, as nothing must detract from the target. This is, of course, how *I* see it. Too, I elected to hold off with any trailing, tailing flash material, exhibiting just a wisp of a top wing. I want the eyes, first and foremost, to be the full focus of attention.

Recipe for Bob B's Black & White Big Bull's-Eye Fly
Saltwater Application

Materials:

> **Hook:** Owner hook. Size 2/0 – black
> **Thread:** Danville's Flat-Waxed Nylon – black
> **Pair of Lady Amherst Pheasant** (white/black-rimmed **tippet feathers**:
>   selected to fit within the periphery of the gap of the hook
> **Eyes:** two, flat, prism tape stick-on (3/8-inch/6.5mm) golden eyes with black
>   pupils
> **Top wing:** white bucktail; black bucktail
> **Epoxy:** five-minute two-part plastic resin epoxy such as Z-Poxy
> **Flex-Seal**
> **Sally Hanson Hard As Nails-With Nylon** (clear nail polish)

Procedure:

1. Using the very tip of your dubbing needle, lightly coat the back of both stick-on eyes with a tad of epoxy and place them just above the black-marked rims of both Lady Amherst pheasant feathers. Press down firmly. Allow to set.

2. When dry, start the wrap of thread directly behind the eye of the hook. Position one of the epoxy-eyed feathers within the periphery of the gap. Align the stem of the feather directly behind the eye of the hook and wrap several times, repositioning if necessary. Repeat the process with the second feather, locking the pair in securely. Trim the stems. A drop of Flex-Seal will secure those wraps quite nicely.

3. For a top wing, mingle and measure a sparse amount of black and white bucktail, which will extend approximately one inch beyond the bend of the hook. Tie in securely behind the eye of the hook

4. Whip finish and lightly epoxy the thread head (allow to dry overnight).

Optional: Apply a dot of Flex Seal to the head. When dry, apply a dot of nail polish to the head. This is more a matter of having you work with these materials, creating a nice glossy finish.

Congratulations are in order, for many of you have completed your first fly. Fish this fly with a stripping action: fast, slow, and everything in between. I have caught several small bass (schoolies) and a few big blues before those eyes were destroyed. Admittedly, it is not a bulletproof fly when attacked; however, it is foolproof. Once you are back home, it is simply a matter of taking a single-edged razor blade and performing radical surgery in order to save the Owner hook and retie the fly. They are excellent hooks—extremely sharp and not cheap. Cheap hooks have no business being part of your terminal tackle. Even as a beginner, once you have epoxied the Mylar eyes onto the Lady Amherst pheasant feathers, you should have no trouble tying a half a dozen of these gems at a clip. Take your time. Don't watch the clock. No one is standing over you. If they are, shoo them away. Also, you may want to experiment by running a thin film of epoxy or an excellent flexible adhesive product called Zap A-Dap-A-Goo II over the surface of the eyes for a bit more durability. That's what this fine hobby will eventually develop into for you: experimentation, innovation and creation. Bob B's Black & White Big Bull's-Eye Fly is my own creation. The fly can be tied in smaller sizes for freshwater applications.

If Electing to Tie Bob B's Black & White Big Bull's-Eye Fly Clouser Style:

In order for a size 2/0 Owner hook (weighing approximately 8 grains) to sink well into the water column, turning itself over properly—that is, upside down in Clouser style—and track well, figure-eight barbell eyes in place after affixing the feathered eyes as instructed in the recipe above. I tie in 20-grain barbell eyes set approximately ¼ inch behind the eye of the hook. The barbell eyes serve solely as a weight—not as eyes.

Note: The barbell eyes should exceed the weight of the hook by at least a two-to-one ratio.

The Gimp
A Fantastic Freshwater Fly

My first fly-tying kit came with a sixty-four page booklet titled *Practical Flies and Their Construction*, written by Lacey E. Gee and Erwin D. Sias, illustrated by John Goettsch (Revised Edition), copyright 1966. I mentioned earlier to shy away from purchasing bargain-priced fly-tying kits. The vise that generally comes with such a kit is usually no bargain; this was true of my original purchase made nearly fifty years ago. In retrospect, however, that little booklet alone was worth the price of the kit. One particular fly recipe instructed readers on how to tie The Gimp, a deadly freshwater fly for trout. I had used that fly successfully for many years on Long Island, fishing the Nissequogue River, Connetquot River and Carmans River, nailing brook, rainbow and brown trout. I played around with the Gimp in ponds and lakes for bluegills and perch. Later in life, I plied the waters of upstate New York and Canada, too. The Gimp is one of my freshwater favorites, rarely having failed me. The fly was Gee's creation. The pattern was initially published in an *Outdoor Life* magazine article titled *They Go for the Gimp*. Interestingly, a good many fly-fishing folks never heard of the fly, while others remember it vaguely. The Gimp is a lethal freshwater fly—a fly that comes along once in a great while.

The magic of the fly is its perfect dun color, simulating many insects.

The Freshwater Gimp

Recipe for the Gimp
Freshwater Application

Materials:

Hook: Mustad-Viking 94838 #8 (turned-down eye)
Thread: Danville's Flat-Waxed Nylon – black
Body: single strand of blue-gray or brown-gray (dun-colored) wool
Tail: several dun-colored hen hackle fibers (toothpick thin)
Wings: two (2) dun-colored Lady Amherst pheasant 'gimp' feathers [found behind, parallel to, just at the base of the larger white, black-rimmed tippet feather].
Collar: one (1) dun-colored hen hackle
Head Cement: Flex-Seal

Procedure:

1. Atop the bend of the hook, tie in several hen hackle fibers to form the tail.

2. Tie in the single strand of dun-colored wool and form a cigar-shaped body, leaving ⅛ inch behind the eye of the hook.

3. For the wings, place and tie in the two gimp feathers, one atop the other, at the head of the tapered body.
    a) Elevate the wings and wrap the thread twice or thrice directly behind the feathers to lock them in a partially raised position.

4. Tie in the dun-colored hen hackle collar, winding it twice around the shank, directly in front of the gimp feather.

5. Trim and whip-finish to the eye of the hook to form the head.

6. Brushing back the collar with the tips of your fingers and holding the fibers out of harm's way, apply the head cement. Allow the thread to absorb the chemical.

Gimp Fly Gone Green
Transition from Freshwater to Saltwater

Many years later, I altered the pattern of the Gimp for saltwater applications, which proved pure dynamite on several species, namely, schoolie-sized bass, big blues and weakfish. In lieu of employing the tiny dun-colored gimp feathers for wings, I selected a pair of metallic green, black-rimmed feathers found just below the neck of the Lady Amherst pheasant. Those lustrous feathers lend an iridescent, insect-like color representative of hoppers and such.

Recipe for Bob B's Green Grabber
Saltwater Application

Materials:

> **Hook:** Owner hook 2/0 (turned-up eye)
> **Thread:** Danville's Flat-Waxed Nylon – black
> **Body:** single two-ply strand of blue-gray or brown-gray (dun-colored) yarn
> **Tail:** several dun-colored hen hackle fibers (matchstick thin)
> **Wings:** two (2) metallic green, black-rimmed plumage from the saddle of the Lady Amherst pheasant
> **Collar:** one (1) dun-colored hen hackle
> **Epoxy:** two-part 5-minute Z-Poxy
> **Sally Hanson Hard As Nails-With Nylon** (clear nail polish)

Procedure:

1. Atop the bend of the hook, tie in several hen hackle fibers to form the tail.

2. Tie in the strands of yarn and form a cigar-shaped body, leaving ⅛ inch behind the eye of the hook.

3. For the wings, place and tie in the two metallic green feathers, one atop the other, at the head of the tapered body.

4. Tie in a dun-colored hen hackle collar, winding it thrice around the shank, directly in front of the feathers.

5. Trim and whip-finish to the eye of the hook to form the head.

6. Brushing back the collar with the tips of your fingers to hold the fibers out of harm's way, apply pinpoints of epoxy to the thread wraps (a little goes a long way). Allow the thread to absorb the chemical.

7. For a glossy head finish after the epoxy has thoroughly dried overnight, carefully coat the head with clear nail polish.

Bob B's Baby (peanut) Bunker

This fly is my variation of the famous Lefty's Deceiver. Few folks have done more for the sport of fly-fishing than Bernard (Lefty) Kreh. It is a privilege for me to present this remarkable fly to you. The success attributed to the fly is three-fold. It has the profile of a baitfish, it casts easily, and it is not prone to fouling.

Bob B's Baby (peanut) Bunker Fly Recipe
Saltwater Application

Materials:

Hook: stainless steel saltwater Mustad-O'Shaughnessy style 3407 ~ 1/0
Thread: Danville's Flat-Waxed Nylon – white
Body: four 2-inch white saddle hackles (two rights and two lefts)
Tail: rainbow Krystal Flash or Flashabou
Underbody: Orvis' 1/8-inch width crosscut rabbit, grizzly or brown
Side Collars: yellow bucktail

Top Wing: pink bucktail

Gills: red flash material

Eyes: gold-rimmed/black pupil; 2.5mm = 5/32-inch flat prism tape stick-on eyes

Sally Hanson Hard as Nails-With Nylon (clear nail polish)

Flex-Seal

Epoxy: five-minute, two-part plastic resin epoxy such as Z-Poxy

Procedure:

1. As a rule of thumb, your saddle hackles should be 1½ times the length of the hook shank. At the bend of the hook, tie in two white saddle hackles [rights], fluff and all, atop the shank, then the other two [lefts]; both pairs facing toward one another rather than splayed outwardly. Cut off excess then half-hitch.

Note: Submerging the feathers in a small bowl of water, then stroking off the excess, will facilitate ease of handling all four feathers simultaneously. Thank you, Lefty Kreh.

2. Tie in approximately five strands of rainbow flash on each side of the feathers. Cut the strands at varying lengths, leaving a few extending no more than ½ inch beyond the length of the tail. You can either tie in one side at a time, or you can take longer lengths, fold them in half and tie in at the same time, manipulating the material to each side.

3. With an approximate 2-inch strip of crosscut rabbit fur positioned upright, its fibers leaning toward the bend of the hook, cut the back strip at an extreme angle to the right. Tie in this tip securely, point facing downward, atop the hook shank by securing it in front of the flash material. Work the thread forward to 3/8-inch behind the eye of the hook, then rotate the rabbit strip in tight connecting wraps to this point. Cut and tie off securely with several half hitches.

4. For the side collars, tie in and secure a small amount of yellow bucktail (less than half the thickness of a wooden matchstick) along both sides of the hook shank, one side at a time, just past the bend in the hook. Wrap securely, forming a nice base for the eyes. Half-hitch.

5. For a top wing, tie in an equal amount of pink bucktail. Tie off and half-hitch.

Note: Selecting hairs from the top two thirds of bucktail, then tying them in lightly with two or three loose wraps—before slowly drawing down steadily with a pinch-wrap in order to hold—not mash the material—will prevent the hairs from flaring. You want the side collars to lie alongside the fur, not flared out like the wings of a B-52 bomber. Too, you want the top wing to rest upon the rabbit hair, not standing erect as if in sheer fright.

6. Turn your fly over in the vise. Cut a small clump of red flash material at an angle. A light brushstroke of nail polish at the end of the fibers will help secure the gill plates in place (¼ inch to the rear and below and the hook eye) as you gently wrap the material and torque down the thread.

7. With your dubbing needle, touch this juncture with a dot of Flex-Seal. Do not allow the opposite end of the flash material to interfere with the gap of the hook.

8. Build up a decent size thread head and whip finish. Cup the eyes, one at a time, by first folding them practically in half in order to fit the form. With the very tip of your dubbing needle, carefully apply a dot of epoxy to the back of one eye, spreading the admixture lightly and evenly across its surface. This will hold it in place for the moment. Repeat for the other eye. A driplet of epoxy applied to the head of the fly, covering both eyes, will make it bulletproof; those wraps will not unravel. Slowly rotate the fly in the vise to be sure the epoxy is spreading evenly. You can easily reposition the eye(s) if need be. You do not want the epoxy to sag, so keep rotating the fly until the epoxy sets and you have a nicely shaped head.

Optional: Allow to dry overnight then apply a dot of clear nail polish for a glossy finish.

Congratulations. You have just constructed a lethal streamer/baby (peanut) bunker fly that tips the Toledo at 10 grains, of which the hook alone weighs 8 grains. It casts like a charm. Fish it with a stripping then a settling motion (pull and positively pause . . . pull and pause), and stand by. Your miniature slayer presents a perfect profile. Study its movement in the water. Take note of the body action referencing the rabbit fur as well as the undulating tail movement. Notice, too, that the water trails off the side collars when the fly is stripped forward.

Bob B's <u>Lengthy</u> 8- to 9-inch, Lethal Streamer/Bunker Fly
Saltwater Application

As big baitfish attract and catch big fish, large artificial flies also attract and catch big fish. Therefore, let's expand upon our Bob B's Baby (peanut) Bunker Fly and create a larger 8- to 9-inch version.

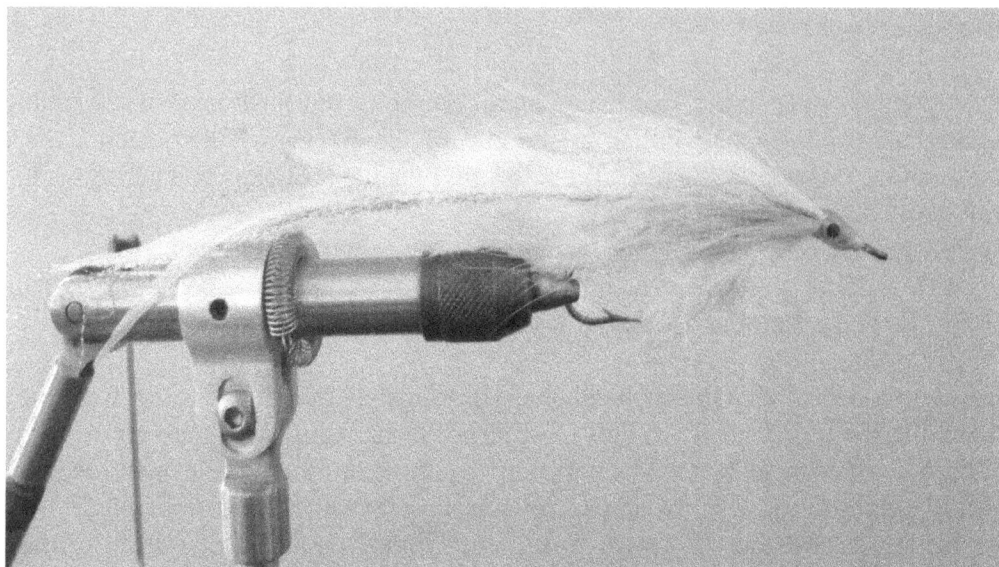

Bob B's Lengthy 8- to 9-inch, Lethal Streamer/Bunker Fly
Saltwater Application

Materials:

> **Hook:** Any quality saltwater 6/0-8XL or 10XL hook (approximately 2¾ inches to 3¼ inches in overall length). An XL (extra-long) designation references the length of the hook shank.

Note: If you have any trouble locating 8XL or 10XL hooks, you may want to contact Mustad, who, back in 1966, acquired Partridge of Redditch Ltd., producers of some of the finest fly hooks in the world. Inquire about Carrie Stevens' 6/0-8XL or 10XL streamer hooks with looped-down eyes and bronze finish. REF CS15.

> **Thread:** Danville's flat waxed nylon – white
> **Body:** eight 5-inch white saddle hackles (four rights and four lefts)
> **Tail:** rainbow Krystal Flash or Flashabou
> **Underbody:** Orvis' 1/8-inch width crosscut rabbit fur in grizzly (grayish white)
> **Side Collars:** yellow bucktail
> **Top Wing:** pink bucktail
> **Eyes:** 3/16-inch prismatic/heliographic gold eyes/black pupils
> **Sally Hanson Hard as Nails-With Nylon** (clear nail polish)
> **Epoxy:** five-minute, two-part plastic resin epoxy such as Z-Poxy

Procedure:

1. As a rule of thumb, your saddle hackles should be 1½ times the length of the hook shank. Approximately ¾ inch behind the eye of the hook, bend the shank down 10 degrees.

2. At the bend of the hook, tie in four 5-inch white saddle hackles [rights], fluff and all, atop the shank, then the other four [lefts], both sets facing toward one another rather than away. Cut off excess then half-hitch.

Note: submerging the feathers in water, then stroking off the excess, will facilitate ease of handling.

3. Tie in approximately five strands of flash on each side of the feathers. Cut the strands at varying lengths, leaving a few extending no more than ½ inch beyond the length of the tail. You can either tie in one side at a time, or you can take longer lengths, fold them in half and tie in at the same time, manipulating the material to each side.

4. With an approximate 4-inch strip of crosscut rabbit fur positioned upright, its fibers leaning toward the bend of the hook, cut the back strip at an extreme angle to the right. Tie in this tip securely, point facing downward, atop the hook shank by securing it in front of the flash material. Work the thread forward to 3/8-inch behind the eye of the hook, then rotate the rabbit strip in tight connecting wraps to this point. Cut and tie off securely with several half hitches.

5. For the side collars, tie in and secure a small bunch of yellow bucktail along both sides of the hook shank.

Note: Selecting hairs from the top two thirds of bucktail, then tying it in with two or three loose wraps—before slowly drawing down firmly—will prevent the hairs from flaring. Once again, as in constructing my Baby (peanut) bunker, you want the side collars to lie alongside the fur, not flared out like the wings of a B-52 bomber. Also, you want the top wing to rest upon the rabbit hair, not standing erect as if in sheer fright.

6. For the top wing, tie in a small bunch of pink bucktail.
    a) No need for gills for this guy. If you so desire, follow steps 6 and 7 in the preceding Baby Bunker recipe.

7. Build up a decent size thread head and whip finish. Cup the eyes, one at a time, by first folding them practically in half in order to fit the form. With the very tip of your dubbing needle, carefully apply a dot of epoxy to the back of one eye, spreading the admixture lightly and evenly across its surface. This will hold it in place for the moment. Repeat for the other eye. A driplet of epoxy applied to the head of the fly, covering both eyes, will make it bulletproof; those wraps will not unravel. Slowly rotate the fly in the vise to be sure the epoxy is spreading evenly. You can easily reposition the eye(s) if need be. You do not want the epoxy to sag, so keep rotating the fly until the epoxy sets and you have a nicely shaped head.

Optional: Allow to dry overnight then apply a dot of clear nail polish for a nice glossy finish.

Congratulations. You have just constructed a lengthy 8- to 9-inch lethal streamer/bunker fly, weighing in at approximately 33 grains, of which the hook alone weighs 23 grains. Fish it as you would my Baby (peanut) Bunker Fly noted in the previous recipe. Your sizable slayer will stand out from the crowd.

Chapter 10

BAITFISH BONANZA ~ THE HERRING FAMILY
LIVE LINING BUNKER & SHAD

As we now move into the bait casting and spin casting realm of angling, it would be a fitting time to mention the types of terminal tackle you'll come across when rigging for saltwater and freshwater species. Terminal tackle is defined as any component attached to the end of your fishing line. For example: monofilament or fluorocarbon leaders, barrel swivels, three-way swivels, sinker snaps, Power Fast Clips, spinner blades, beads and, of course, hooks.

Types of Hooks

You will hear and read about **Sproat** bend type hooks. These are simply fishhooks having a circular bend, named after W. H. Sproat, a 19th-century English angler. **Circle** type hooks are more C-shaped, designed for healthy catch and release, hooking the fish in the corner of its mouth rather than having it gut-hooked. **J-shaped** hooks are just that—shaped like a J. **Beak** type hooks commonly refer to the point of the hook, sometimes called a rolled-in point. This style hook has the point bent inward toward the shank of the hook. Though the hook, in and of itself, takes a smaller bite because of a shorter gap (distance between hook point and shank), it has excellent holding power. A fish is less likely to dislodge itself. An **O'Shaughnessy** designed hook is forged with a relatively thick, strong bend. It is a standard saltwater hook, especially for bottom fishing. **Aberdeen** hooks are generally made from shaped wire. Unlike the O'Shaughnessy, an Aberdeen type hook can bend; albeit, once a fish is hooked and the barb has completely penetrated, this hook holds quite well. Aberdeen hooks are mainly for light freshwater fishing. A **Treble** hook is three hooks brazed together (along their shanks) to form a single hook. The hook is used to either hook a fish in the mouth or snag it. The latter method generally employs a weighted treble hook.

Let's examine a couple of techniques for taking *big* fish—especially bluefish and bass caught with live baitfish. As a generally accepted maxim, *big* fish love and seek out *big* bait. Bunker is one of a predator's favorite baitfish.

Casting a 1½ ounce weighted treble hook in order to snag menhaden (a.k.a bunker, mossbunker or pogies—not porgies) is a surefire way to score with monster blues and behemoth bass. The idea is to snag a number of live bunker and live line the baitfish so as to catch big blues and bass. Not surprisingly, quite often, when retrieving a wounded, writhing bunker through a watery—perhaps bloody—path to the boat, a prodigious predator will aggressively attack your crippled catch. Donna and I have nailed many a nice size fish in this fashion. Where bunker, shad and other good-sized baitfish abound, you are bound to meet up with a notable prize, if not a trophy.

There are basically three ways in which to live line baitfish: through the nose, in front of the second dorsal fin, or in the tail. When Donna and I drift fish, our preferred method of live lining baitfish, be it bunker or shad, is to insert a 4/0 hook in front of the second dorsal fin. This hook placement will allow the baitfish to swim deep. Applying sporadic thumb pressure upon the spool of a baitcasting reel will cause the baitfish to struggle erratically, sending out a series of vibrations, vibrations that signal predators that an injured fish—easy pickings—is in the area.

Keep in mind that *big* striped bass hang low in the water column, allowing their smaller brothers and sisters to feast on a school of baitfish fleeing above them. Hooking a baitfish through the nose will cause it to swim high in the water column. It would then become necessary to tie in a sinker to either a dropper loop or a three-way swivel in order to hold the weighted creature closer to the bottom. Why bother with an added line and different weight sinkers to match a specific current? Why complicate the issue? Lunker bass are the laziest of the lot and will often wait for a wounded or dead bunker to descend. When bluefish, mixed in with schooling bass, rip through an area with a vengeance, it is the wise-old linesiders that lie in wait for an easy target and meal.

For conventional medium-heavy and heavy-duty work, such as jigging and trolling the deeper waters of Long Island Sound, I employ either 20- to 30-pound test monofilament or lead core line, respectively. That is when I rig baitfish differently by running a larger hook, such as a 6/0, through the top jaw and out an eye socket. If added weight is needed, I'll incorporate an in-line drail-style sinker. The reels we employ are venerable Penn reels: Donna's model 99 is spooled with monofilament; my Senator 4/0 Special is spooled with lead core. Those reels are paired with wands so old that the labeling has been worn away. They will eventually be retired and replaced with a pair of complementing Ugly Stiks. All told, you simply cannot beat these rods. You can beat them up, but you can't kill them.

Although blues and bass love fresh *live* baitfish, bunker and other prospective victims are not always around for the taking when you're ready to play. Therefore, the game becomes a matter of catch-as-catch-can: snagging, killing then immediately freezing baitfish for later use will prove wise.

Working a section of shoreline of the Peconic River on April 30th, 2008, I had to cast a weighted treble hook a considerable distance in order to snag the two dozen bunker that I'd later use for bait to carry me through the spring season. Those related cousins of the herring clan were hunkered down midway between the two shorelines. It was 6 p. m., three hours before high tide. Every cast produced at least a foot long bunker, which told me that they were out there in significant numbers—moving back and forth throughout the water column: bottom, middle, and near the top. Nothing appeared to be chasing them. Satisfied with a couple dozen, I froze all but two for the following morning, figuring I'd try for some serious bass sporting broad shoulders instead of the 16- to 19-inch schoolies I'd been playing around with on a fly rod since the third week in April. I surmised that it was probably still too early in the season, as mid-May is usually magic time for lunker bass. I knew I'd certainly have the opportunity to mix it up with some big blues now that the bunker were in the area. I had no idea at that moment how prolific the bunker bonanza would be.

I awoke early on the morning of May 1st to a sight I shall not forget. I wouldn't have needed a weighted treble hook to snag bunker from the center of the river. I could have scooped them up at the shoreline with a bucket. Three hours before high tide in the a. m., as far as the eye could see—east and west and across the entire river—the dorsal fins and tails of a guesstimated tens of thousands of bunker were swimming erratically in all directions. Many were floating or flapping upon the surface, dead or half dead, oxygen starved after bluefish in the 30-inch plus category had driven them upriver and corralled them in downtown Riverhead. As it turned out, local experts estimated that *hundreds of thousands* of bunker had entered the river and its tributaries. A neighbor had nailed nine monster blues the evening before, excitedly telling me that one of those brutes stood end to end with several inches of its tail sticking above the rim of a thirty-two gallon galvanized container. The neighbor's home is a stone's throw from the river, and the man witnessed scores of folks catching these choppers on virtually every cast.

East of the Route 105 Bridge in Flanders Bay and Great Peconic Bay, Donna and I caught several tackle busters on poppers and Kastmasters. Next, I wanted to give myself a challenge, so I set up a fly rod with the serious 9-inch bunker fly covered in the preceding chapter. Four more beasts succumbed to the deadly pattern before I was wasted. I brought gigantic fresh fillets to friends and neighbors who truly appreciated my first significant catch of the season while Donna and I patiently awaited those coveted bass to arrive en masse.

Bunker Kill Along the Peconic River Shoreline

As temperatures rose through the week, so did the stench. It got pretty funky around our property with the wind coming out of the south. I had never seen so many seagulls surveying the area—morning, noon and night. I think the ospreys were replete if not hunkered down in their nests with bellyaches. As the tides changed, many of us folks were out there along the shoreline with boat poles and other implements, freeing hundreds upon hundreds of dead bunker from behind our bulkheads as well as the reeds. The remaining bunker submerged beneath our dock would just have to wait until Mother Nature took its course. The upshot would be a great crabbing season some optimists had predicted, while realists knew that decaying fish lying on the bottom of the river use up oxygen and would have a negative effect.

For the weeks that followed, I was one of several folks wearing a disposable mask, busy cutting the grass, trimming the hedges, weed whacking the periphery of our property, and positioning my leaf blower in a definite southerly direction. While on the water, I wore a bandanna stretched across my nose and mouth. I told myself that if the river still reeked in weeks to come, I would place a temporary name across the stern of my vessel: *EAU DE BUNKER*.

Bunker Kill Revisited

No sooner than us North Fork folks had witnessed and endured an historic, massive bunker kill of an estimated half a million adult menhaden at the end of April, 2008, a second wave of 13-inch bunker were found floating or flapping upon the surface—dead or half dead. Their bodies lined the shores of the Peconic River and area bays from Riverhead out east to Mattituck. From April 30th into the beginning of June, the stench of decaying fish filled the air. Those of us who reside along the river, creeks and bays had put our friends' visits, family barbecues, picnics and other planned outings on hold, lest our guests be put off from the sheer smell. Good-sized bluefish, some 30 inches and 10 pounds plus, had once again chased and corralled the bunker into the backwater behind Main Street in Riverhead.

While waiting for those behemoth bass to show, I wrote a poem for a very special reason and season. As many of us complained bitterly about the bunker invasion, I took a moment to look on the positive side—about what these prolific creatures truly provide. I have tremendous respect for bunker, for they are a vital source in the food chain. Few folks realize just how important bunker are, not only to the marine fisheries but to several other industries as well. Let's note just how important they are by way of this ode, keeping firmly in mind that I'm a novelist and an outdoors writer, not a poet.

ODE TO MENHADEN

By Robert Banfelder

Menhaden are an oily fish,
Members of the Clupeidae class,
Unquestionably a bony dish,

Alas—as table fare, I'll pass.
Monikered as bunkers,
Mossbunkers and pogies, too,
Best served up whole for choppers and lunkers,
Or ladled as chum by a crew.

Man-eating sharks shall follow,
This slick in search of a meal,
And if their stomachs prove hollow,
Shall swallow—hook, line, sinker and reel.
So, too, the old salt behind it,
Half asleep in a fish-fighting chair,
Ere the rod split, the poor soul took a fit,
Vanishing into thin air.

Food for thought that bunker are magnets,
Enticing all sizes that swim,
As cited, should you remain stagnant,
You could soon lose your shirt or your skin.
Melville and Mundus have stories,
Both with whales of a tale to tell,
Scribing their ghostly Great White glories,
But 'twas bunker that raised them from hell.

Landlubbers prize bunker for gardens,
As fertilizer for farmers to grow,
Producers fill bags, crates and cartons,
It's big business for those in the know.
As pet food, it's surely a winner,
Puss 'n Boots truly will trip,
Duke and Lassie shall lunge for their dinner
Kittylina swears it's catnip.

A public stink could certainly be ended.
Simply close off its nose with a clip,
And for those who still are offended,
Should try working a processing ship,
Which carries a crew and its measure,
Worth its weight in silver and gold,
Treasures for work, health, beauty and pleasure,
Forty-four byproducts all-told.

Sport drinks,
Salad dressings,
Perfumes,

Sauces
& Soup ~
Inks,
Resins,
Varnishes
& Linoleum ~
Lipsticks to continue the loop.

Widely varied, its uses are many,
First as oils for machinery and tools.
Omega 3 now at one pretty penny,
Being but one of its bright crowning jewels.
Whether of peanut-sized dimension,
Or firmly and fully mature,
Menhaden are quite the attention,
Of fishes, yes—but still to too few folks allure.

This lyric poem was inspired by Herman Melville's *Moby Dick* and Frank Mundus' *Sportfishing for Sharks* as well as *Fifty Years a Hooker*.

Respectively, snagging or cast netting live bunker provides recreational as well as commercial fishermen the opportunity to score big. Bonkers over Bunker (menhaden) = Behemoth Blues & Bass

Somersaulting Over Shad

Of course, bunker are not the only baitfish in the sea. It was near the end of October in 2003. Donna and I were fishing the Peconic River, between the Route 105 Bridge and Russ Moran's Indian Island Clubhouse Restaurant in Riverhead. We were working a medium-action spinning outfit and a fly rod: she with 10-pound test monofilament carrying a ¾-ounce Kastmaster; me with a fast-sinking shooting head trailing a Clouser Minnow—a deadly fly on many species. I was hooking up like there was no tomorrow, but losing many more fish than I landed. Donna nailed a couple with her tin but then lost them, too. We switched rods. Those silvery green specters simply vaulted high into the misty air then vanished instantly, presumably spitting our hooks as we threw a series of sissy fits. Initially, we believed we were into a school of bunker. But we also knew that bunker do not blast flies or lures with a vengeance—or at all! Something was surely fishy. We figured that those puzzlements belonged to something in the herring family; but what exactly? Admittedly, that day was certainly confusing to us, and with good reason, for we had only recently made the transition from freshwater fly-fishing (for brookies, browns and rainbow trout) to saltwater fly-fishing (for stripers, blues and weakfish), apart from baitfish being part of the bargain.

The year before, same month and in that very same spot—the two of us throwing Kastmasters—we had inadvertently snagged scores of menhaden. We hooked them in the back, the tail, the belly. Therefore, this time around, we initially thought we were into a school of the same baitfish. But why were they striking our lures head on and hard—on both the Kastmaster and the Clouser Minnow? We later learned that what we were hooking were hickory shad, not menhaden. Wild, flying-out-of-the-water acrobatic show-offs. Fun. Fun. Fun. Like miniature tarpon those torpedoes ascended and broke the surface straightaway. Donna duped several with the Kastmaster. I caught better than a dozen with the fly. Still, in all truthfulness, we lost many more than we actually landed. But why? Subsequent research revealed the answer. Like weakfish, hickory shad have thin, tissue paper-like mouths. They are to be played very gently; most carefully. And forget about trying to lift them out of the water by lure or leader.

At an Eastern Flyrodders of Long Island meeting, I had broached the dubious shad/bunker subject with Mark Sedotti, a veteran fly caster. He told me about a book and an old friend of his: Joe Brooks' *Salt Water Fly Fishing*. Joe was editor for *Outdoor Life* from 1968 to 1972, the year he passed away. Mark and I discussed American shad, hickory shad, bunker and other such species. Additionally, Tom Cousins, a longtime member of the club and past president of the Salty Flyrodders of New York, made mention of Lefty Kreh's works. Lefty is a living legend (who I certainly mentioned earlier) and author of dozens of books on the subject of fly-fishing, covering both fresh and salt water.

Off to the library and bookstore for references covering chapter and verse concerning those aerial acrobats in order to help clear away the cobwebs often surrounding the enigma regarding members of the herring family. Between Joe Brooks and Lefty Kreh, I had a pretty good idea how Donna and I could consistently hook and land these celestial leapers in the future, pledging to return all but a few to the waters for purposes of later live lining these great baitfish. I learned that hickory shad do not make fine table fare as explained by folks I spoke with as well as through books written by those over whose pages I poured. Cookbooks included.

Succinctly, this is what I gleaned: American shad (*Alosa sapidissima*), which is prized for its roe and praised by only a small number of folks for its flesh, can be found along both sides of Long Island Sound, especially near the Connecticut River. Hickory shad (*Pomolobus mediocris*), however, do not receive such accolades, unless you are into pet food, fertilizer, chum, or live lining as mentioned. According to James Peterson, award-winning cookbook writer (*Fish & Shellfish*), most people generally shy away from eating American shad because of all the tiny bones, yet the author remains dauntless, emphatically stating that it is a delicious fish. Nowhere can I find anyone who condescends in accepting its cousin, ol' hickory, as acceptable cuisine.

Opinions and arguments set aside, Donna and I can tell you firsthand that we had a fantastic afternoon enjoying the aerial antics of those 18-inch anadromous (migrating from salt water to spawn in fresh water) acrobats.

For purposes of identification, note that hickory shad are smaller than their counterpart; that is, three and a half pounds tops versus 6 to 8 pounds; 18 inches versus 30 inches, respectively. Also, the lower jaw of the hickory shad protrudes past the upper jaw while the mandible of the American shad closes evenly. This is the best way to distinguish the pair. Between menhaden and hickory shad, the picture may seem somewhat murky to the neophyte. So rather than get into confusing colors and questionable body markings, bunker simply will not take your lure nor give you an acrobatic show. Anglers will merely snag them—inadvertently or otherwise. In any event, you do not want hickory shad on the menu as the Catch of the Day, or any day. And certainly not mossbunker, God forbid! Still, either species acting as a magnet for a 13-plus-pound bluefish or the two 32-inch stripers that Donna and I landed a week later via live lining will certainly draw us out in search of those aerial acrobats in seasons to come.

Squid & Mummichogs (to be discussed in Chapter 12 under Fluke)

From the middle of October 2012, right up until the moment Hurricane Sandy threatened then hit our coastline not two weeks later, our westerly North Fork bays were replete with ¾-inch peanut bunker as well as 13- to 14- inch adults. You could ostensibly, once again, traverse our westerly North Fork bays upon the backs of those adults. The influx of menhaden initially seemed reminiscent of the spring bunker kill of 2008. Thankfully, this time around, it didn't come to that. Still, with the number of bunker around our area bays, Donna and I did not score as well with big blues and bass as we had in past seasons, but not for a lack of trying. We tried several methods: live lining, chunking, sending down clam bellies well into the water column, finally plugging and tossing tins. Too much bait for those predators was listed as one of a number of excuses.

Chris Paparo with a brace of bluefish

Occasional monsters blues were landed, such as Chris Paparo's choppers, headed for the smoker. However, most of us fishing fools, Chris included, were targeting big bass. "That's why they call it fishing," was the rhetorical lament repeated when those linesiders were not cooperating.

The forewarning of news reports referencing Hurricane Sandy prompted Donna and I to haul our boat early that season. Better safe than sorry. I topped off the tank (leaving room for expansion), changed the oil and hauled out our center console. As Sandy took her leave, Donna and I were relegated to our kayak, canoe and inflatable. Not a problem as we've caught many a prize in the late fall and even into winter with those smaller crafts. You have to, of course, dress properly. As heavy rains diluted the salinity of the suds and drove the bunker south, we went to plan B.

The downstairs chest freezer was one-quarter filled with fresh frozen menhaden for any holdover blues and/or bass. On October 29, a full moon coupled with already high tides added to the threat of 'The Perfect Storm.' We prayed that we wouldn't lose electricity for any significant length of time. Otherwise, I'd be cooking up a storm for friends and boating neighbors at our nearby marina: venison harvested during Calverton's 2012 bow and arrow season, goose breasts from last gunning season, along with this year's abundance of porgies, blowfish, sea bass, a few weakfish and several striped bass steaks—we do not freeze bluefish, although you certainly can.

Chapter 11

LETHAL LURES FOR SALT & FRESH WATER

Veteran outdoors writer and consummate angler William "Doc" Muller drives home an important point. "If you want to learn how to fish bucktails [jigs] effectively, fish nothing but bucktails." Donna and I subscribe to that sort of reasoning, having jigged bucktails trailing Uncle Josh's pork strips for a good number of years. It's a wonderful lure/bait combo. Also, Storm's WildEye holographic soft plastics from four to six inches prove quite deadly. Additionally, in our saltwater/freshwater arsenal, we are well-armed with a favorite tried-and-true 'killer' tin—the Kastmaster, ranging from 1/12-to 4-ounce weights. It is our go-to spinning lure. All these lures have produced remarkably well for us.

Then along came a female member of Eastern Flyrodders at 5 a. m. on May 4th of 2007. Donna set our guest up for some schoolies with a medium-action rod and ½-ounce Kastmaster. The three of us were working Kastmasters off the stern of my vessel, *Write On*. It was approximately three hours after high tide; the water was moving at its max on the Peconic River. Perfect! Donna and I usually clobber those shorts with that tin, but not so effectively that morning. After a couple dozen casts, our guest politely said that she wanted to switch to her new rod and reel, along with her own lure. Her tin looked a tad too heavy for the column of water we were fishing, but each to his or her own.

On the woman's first cast with her new spinning outfit, she hooked a nice 16-inch schoolie. Long story short, she outfished yours truly by a two-to-one ratio. She outfished Donna five-to-one. With an envious eye, I kept looking at that somewhat familiar lure. Seemingly from thin air, our guest pulled out a duplicate tin.

"Here," she offered through a winsome smile, passing the lure before us.

Donna and I both declined. I removed the Kastmaster and tied on a 4-inch holographic Storm WildEye Swim Shad—Shiner Chartreuse Silver. It rarely fails me. Our guest's demonstration of one-upmanship went on for a good part of the morning before she offered the lure a second time. This time I folded after Donna politely declined, stubbornly sticking to her favorite lure: the Kastmaster.

"Yes," I said, smiling inwardly, greedily but carefully grabbing the tin.

Suddenly, I was in on our guest's steady action. Most magically we were catching small but feisty schoolies. I wasn't going to catch up with our guest's runaway record, but I was a happy soul. We fished until the tide dropped and the bite was off. For years I had seen that sleek, tapered tin advertised in all the fishing magazines and displayed on the racks in most tackle shops, but I couldn't for the life of me recall its name.

"What's the name of that lure?" I surely had to ask.

"Why, that's my *Deadly Dick*," she answered, grinning mischievously.

"Uh huh," was my only comeback.

The two ladies had a good laugh, and our guest made me a gift of a 4-inch Deadly Dick #2 long; silver on one side, blue on the other. After we all enjoyed breakfast that morning and our guest headed home, I immediately went off to my local tackle shop—Edward's Sports Center in Riverhead—hoping that Diane, Ron's better half and business partner, didn't keep them hidden behind the counter whereby I'd have to announce my request in a *whisper.*

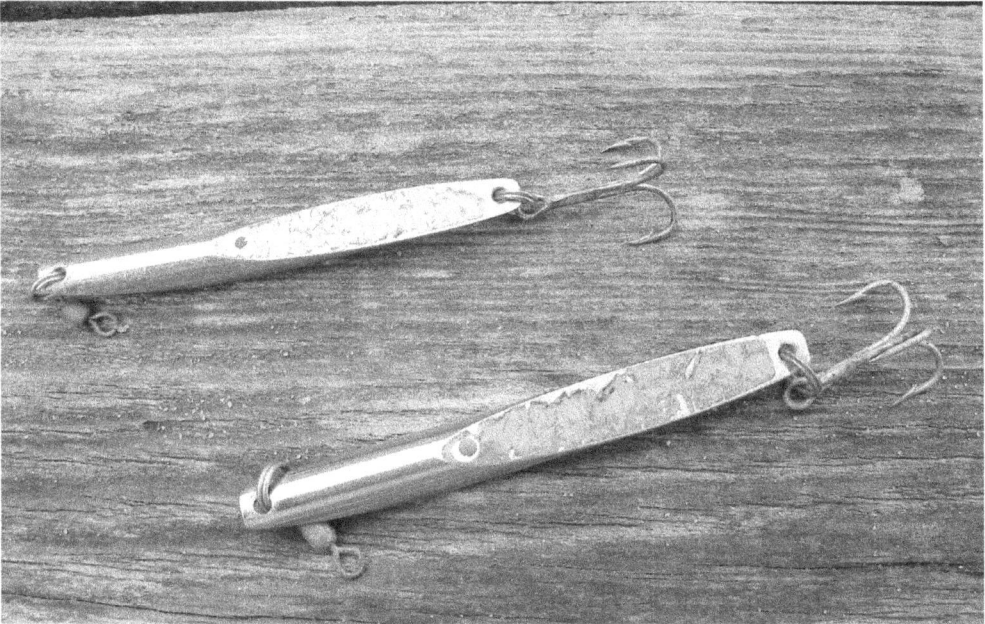

Deadly Dick Lures

Try these lures in silver/blue, silver/green, and silver/white; they're winners.

In general, I'm a creature of habit and a proponent of, "If it ain't broke, don't fix it." However, I'm not closed-minded. If I believe that I can build a better mousetrap or improve upon its design, I'll certainly give it a whirl. Following that early morning episode with our guest and her Deadly Dick lure, having upstaged both Donna and me while wielding our trusty Kastmasters, we had asked ourselves why in the world had the woman's lure outperformed ours—and by such a significant margin? Whereas the Kastmaster has a more or less oval peanut bunker shape to it, the Deadly Dick has a streamlined spearing or sand lance-like appearance. As peanut bunker show up in the fall, and it was now early May, I figured that a school of good-sized minnows had arrived, preferring our guest's 4-inch imitation rather than accepting Donna's and my 2¼-inch appetizer offerings. But I truly questioned whether those omnivorous schoolies had been that selective, preferring one shape and/or size over the other, and with such consistency, especially since they had been given a two-to-one presentment that morning; that is, Donna's and my Kastmasters versus our guest's single lure.

I held to an idea as to what might actually have transpired that fine morning. The clarity of the water had been especially apparent. I know from experience that artificial flies affixed with eyes far exceed hook-up ratios than those imitations that do not sport peepers. Had our eyeless 'go-to' lures suddenly let us down for no apparent reason? Was I blindly casting doubt? The Deadly Dick lure that our guest had sent into the suds sported a single red and white eye. Could that have been it—one eye being better than none? Or was it that our guest had inadvertently or otherwise matched the hatch concerning those selective stripers (although we hadn't seen a single baitfish)? Retrieved through the water column, our guest's thin strip of metal may have flashed and silently communicated, "Predator fish, here is your target, complete with bull's-eye. Catch me if you can." So why not add pairs of eyes to those saltwater tins that Donna and I love to launch?

And what about the 4-inch holographic Storm WildEye Swim Shad I had used, too, that morning? I claimed that it rarely failed me. Yet, it had. I dug it out of my tackle bag and examined its eyes. They were barely discernible. Time, tide and several takers had taken their toll. The lure should have been retired, refurbished or trashed.

I immediately put my energy into fine-tuning our eyeless Kastmasters. With a drop of epoxy, I simply glued a pair of flat 3/16-inch prismatic/heliographic gold eyes with black pupils to the Kastmaster.

The next morning my hook-up ratio went up instantly. It is interesting to note, too, that Donna, fishing right alongside of me with another 2½-inch, ½-ounce but eyeless Kastmaster, had about the same hook-up ratio as when the two of us fished with our guest but a day earlier. Then something struck me! No, not Donna's lure, but another thought. Donna's Kastmaster, as did mine, came dressed with white bucktail tied to the treble hook. Everything was the same, including our retrieve. Our guest's Deadly Dick tin did not have bucktail attached to the treble hook. Still, she had outfished us.

Experience has taught me, too, that bucktail undulating through the water column, whether in the form of a fly or fixed to a lure, gives the angler the added edge. I studied the Kastmaster's limited tail action moving through the suds. What if I were to fashion a slightly longer tail? Not too long, but just a tad longer to give the tail a bit more action. Too, I could pick the color(s) of my choice. Whereas lures and flies with orbs will outproduce those that turn a blind eye, so too will tail action up your score.

This was by no means a one or two day trial test, but rather a full season of experimentation: Kastmasters fixed with eyes and left without eyes; those very tins with and without tails; tails tied with longer bucktail; others tied with marabou. The only problem being, which one of us was going to receive the short end of the stick, Donna or I? As there can only be one captain . . . well, I think you get my drift. I outproduced Donna by a considerable ratio. When we finally did switch rods and lures, after mutiny was about to be declared, Donna ran away with the program.

Think about how you can alter some of your tins, plugs, spinners, flies, et cetera. You will be limited only by your imagination. Where do you begin? Start by flipping a coin; heads or tails. Either way you're sure to be a winner.

Recipe for Altering Kastmasters (as well as other tins) Covering Saltwater and Freshwater Applications

Materials:
>   **Kastmaster (or other eyeless tins)**

Note: Cabela's (outdoor outfitters) sells Kastmaster nickel-plated knockoffs identified as "Dressed Casting Spoons," as well as plain "Casting Spoons" for considerably less money. They work just as well as the Acme Tackle Co. original.

>   **Thread:** color choice is yours
>   **Eyes:** pairs of either flat or three-dimensional 3/16-inch prismatic/heliographic gold eyes with black pupils; also, green with black pupils (adhesive or non-adhesive back)
>   **Epoxy:** Z-Poxy (five-minute two-part–hardener/resin)
>   **Toothpicks**
>   **Bodkin**
>   **Tail:** bucktail or marabou–color choice is yours

Procedure:

1. Set the lure on a flat surface.

2. With the very tip of your dubbing needle, carefully apply a dot of epoxy to the back of one eye, spreading the admixture lightly and evenly across its surface. With the end of a toothpick, touch and lift the eye, placing and gently pressing it down upon the lure until the epoxy reaches and lines the very edge of the eye's rim. Allow the eye to set for an hour.

3. Once dry, turn the lure over and complete the other side.

4. Along the shank of the treble hook, between each division, tie in a small bunch of either bucktail or marabou material. Epoxy the wraps.

Tins that come with tails can be left alone until they get chewed up to the point that they are no longer effective. I then redress them by making the tail slightly longer than the original. Bucktail dressing tied on Kastmasters fashioned with single hooks I find adequate, so when I do repair them, I keep the material the same length as the original. Personally, for greater insurance, I prefer treble hooks rather than single hooks affixed to my tins. Granted, that when the bite is on, it is much easier to remove a single hook from a fish's mouth than it is to fuss and fumble with a treble hook. However, I like the insurance factor over the convenience component. But that's just me.

When it's time to redress tackle, do not shy away from being creative. Adding a pair of eyes will blindside your opponent. Experiment, too, by tying in bucktail, marabou, and/or other feathers in order to give color and action to your favorite spoons, spinners, plugs, et cetera. Doing so may surprise both you and your quarry.

Black Beauty
Clearly a Crankbait Winner

Hurricane Sandy left our westerly North Fork area bays high but shy of bunker. Hence, the bite was off. The ospreys had left for better hunting grounds, and an American Bald Eagle took its place, sitting perched upon the fish hawks' vacant nest along Colonel's Island, just east of the 105 Bridge in Riverhead. Christopher Paparo (marine biologist, fisherman, columnist, hunter, falconer and wildlife photographer) put aside rod and reel, grabbed his kayak and camera then headed east along the Peconic River with high hopes of capturing photos of our nation's emblematic treasure. Chris got a quick shot or two as the eagle was suddenly spooked by a fisherman with a cast net in hand, looking for any sign of bunker. No great shot of the bird of prey for Chris, no bunker for the fisherman, and no fish around for the eagle or any angler—or so I had thought.

80

I was ready to pack it in for the season. The 18-foot center console had been put to bed the day before the storm. In its stead sat my 7-foot, 9-inch inflatable, just in case I saw some action or heard some positive reports. I had gone out a few times but with very little luck—and that is after having thrown out everything I could muster in the hope of hooking up. I made offerings of tins, jigs, soft plastics, spinners, poppers; flies both large and small; clam bellies and frozen bunker strips. I was targeting anything with significant shoulders with which I could proudly close the season. *Nada*. Needless to say, I felt a bit frustrated.

What to do?

I figured I'd try the complete opposite of what Donna and I usually do. I'd invert the process. What did I really have to lose? As I had already fished the early mornings and late evenings with not so much as a touch or a tap, having purposely picked a mid-tide with the flow of water moving along nicely, I now decided to fish the early afternoon during a dead-calm low. Both my experience and logbook tell me that moving water and/or dusk to dawn pursuits are best for big bass. Therefore, if I were going to purposely do things *wrong*, I might just as well get it *right*. Right?

After repeating the program described above, once again exhausting my arsenal, I selected a long black jointed lure that I had forgotten about for several seasons. The color black I usually reserve for nighttime fishing. However, in keeping with my nonsensical plan of action, I set up a Shimano Sustain 5000 FE reel coupled to a Shakespeare SP 1101 7-foot Medium-Heavy action rod then clipped on the lure: a 7-inch jointed black Bomber model #16J-Magnum Long "A". It is a deadly lure for stripers and blues. Too, it has proven lethal on pike, pickerel as well as large and smallmouth bass. Therefore, it *was* my go-to plug pick for both sweetwater and the suds. But with all the new crankbaits I've experimented with over the course of years, I had passed over this winner. It had been tucked away in my surf bag.

I started out trolling the south shoreline of Flanders Bay, rowing the inflatable while running the lure through a stretch of shallow murky water, the artificial minnow alternately diving between a foot and eighteen inches. Suddenly, the rod tip bent. I released the oars, grabbed the rod, and reeled in a submerged branch with several leaves attached.

Maneuvering the craft about, I headed for deeper water, trailing the red-eyed, black-bodied crankbait through a 3-foot column. Suddenly, there came another bend in the rod. I reached for it and felt the fish grab then let go of the lure; enough trolling for the moment. I sent the one-ounce body sailing, watching the lure splash and settle before retrieving it slowly; it wiggled lifelike as it neared the surface. My third twenty-five-yard cast resulted in a solid hit. A minute or so later, I landed a nice fat 20-inch linesider.

Within the first hour, I released two more stripers—20 and 23 inches. No keepers, but I was pleased . . . somewhat.

I thought a lot about that tapered streamlined lure, hanging there before me at the ready as I rowed to another corner of the same shoreline. Seven inches long when you figure in its hardware: hangers, split rings and ¾-inch clear plastic front-fixed lip, configured to run shallow on a slow and steady retrieve—made to dive deeper into the water column with an aggressive reeling action set against the short-nosed diving plane. Two 1/0 treble hooks: one positioned at its furthermost rear section, the other placed just forward of center of the front section. Over the course of years, the plug proved to be sheer dynamite—from Gananoque along the St. Lawrence River, through Maine and other New England waters, right on down along our coastline. Salt water or fresh water, it repeatedly took nice fish.

At $9, the lure is a bargain that is hard to beat—hard being the operative word. The body's polycarbonate modulus tensile strength rating is 350,000, which translates into 1,200 pounds of hydraulic pressure being applied before the lure would shatter. That's some serious force. Muskies may certainly make their mark upon those Bombers, and big bluefish will absolutely batter them, but you cannot kill that lure. What can happen is that you can lose the crankbait in the heat of battle if you're not careful, so I advise using a wire leader, especially when tackling those toothy predators. I don't always follow my own advice, but I pass it along anyway.

The wounded artificial baitfish swimming action of the Bomber 16J–Magnum Long "A" is long on performance and short on patience in attracting predators. During the next hour, I had caught and released three more of those linesiders in Flanders Bay, for a total of six shorties.

If there is a lesson to be learned from all of this, and there most certainly is, it's to try and not get locked into a regimented approach but rather to experiment with what may even be considered an unorthodox reach. Initially, nothing was working for me. Not even fresh frozen bait such as clam and bunker. Go figure. I had worked several of my favorite proven lures and patterns during a tide that had almost always produced for me; that is, maximum current. But by inverting the whole ball of wax, so to speak, I worked the black-colored crankbait usually set aside for nighttime fishing, fished it during daylight hours in lieu of the preferred dust to dawn approach for targeting stripers, then hooked into, landed and released a half dozen linesiders in a couple of hours. It was the only lure in my assortment that produced. I'll remind you of that age old adage, and that is: "That's why they call it fishing."

Admittedly, I was a tad disappointed that I didn't come away with dinner. A couple of fillets would have been nice for the table. I'll just bet that beautiful American Bald Eagle had no trouble scoring a meal spied from its outpost. Of course, those birds of prey have no restrictions other than the weight of what they can carry away in their talons; an awesome sight to behold!

Chapter 12

FLUKE FISHING GARDINERS TO THE GREENLAWNS

Tackle, Bait (Squid & Mummichogs), Tactics

The waters surrounding Long Island offer some of the best fluking this side of Paradise. Paradise defined, of course, as a place where flatties are so prodigious that tape measures become unnecessary because every fish falls well within the legal limit. Even bag limits may take on a literal meaning as every fisherman has one fashioned from burlap, which at day's end is filled to capacity since quotas are a thing of a past life, too. Then again, one wouldn't dare call it fishing but something more along the lines of an everyday catching occurrence as things are that easy in Eden. However, until we hopefully arrive, arising to that time and place, we mortals must contend with size limits, bag limits, seasonal restrictions and weather conditions whether we like it or not while we're down here fishing up a storm. Therefore, if you haven't thrown away your measuring tape yet or ran out to try and locate one of those antiquated bags of jute or hemp used in days gone by, having returned to finish this paragraph after realizing I'd set your hopes too high, being the antsy optimist that you are, I'll try my damnedest to put you next to nirvana. Where? Gardiners Bay, then a run down to the west side of Shelter Island to the Greenlawns.

You'll truly believe you died and went to heaven. Even the names Gardiners Bay and the Greenlawns might conjure up some sort of empyrean right here on earth . . . either that or a final resting place. In any event, rest assured that the action is going to be hot from the middle of May through June, for openers. Then, as the season progresses, I'll direct you to areas that will produce fat flatties into September. Am I guiding you to the nautical equivalent of the Promised Land? You better believe it—with pictures to prove it and the infallible word of my terrestrial angel, Donna.

With a bit of whimsy set aside, Donna is dead serious when it comes to fishing. Too, she is patience personified. For example, during a Fourth of July holiday in 2004, Donna and I climbed aboard an acquaintance's serious fishing vessel named *Finally*. The captain had invited Donna along, thinking that my soul mate would prove a good companion for his wife, daughter and her boyfriend, as it was to be an all-day excursion. *Finally* is a good-size vessel with lots of cockpit room. The space that Donna occupied from sunrise to sunset, with an occasional break from hauling in fluke after skate after fluke, was at the stern of that Baha Cruiser. Donna found and settled into her own little corner off to starboard of that 11½ foot beamed beauty. It wasn't that Donna was being in any way rude. It was simply that she was having the time of her life, learning, for the first time, how to *really* catch fluke. It wasn't her first time fluke fishing, mind you. Nor was it mine. It's just that we didn't have the knack or know-how to excel. Luck was slowly being transformed into lore. Donna was pulling in flatties hand over fist, mastering the art under the tutelage of Captain Carl Schnitter, fluke fisherman *extraordinaire*. To put it plainly, Carl is accomplished, patient and personable.

Concerning our lessons, there were conditions set forth by Carl. Both Donna and I were sworn to secrecy: secrecy as to the 'secret weapon' we'd be employing; secrecy as to how the rig was fashioned; secrecy with regard to technique; and especially secrecy with respect to the precise spots we fished. Donna and I take secrets very seriously. We can be trusted. We'll take those confidences to the grave. We, too, have fishing secrets of our own. Occasionally, we share a secret or two—never secrets entrusted to us, upon which we had sworn an oath, but rather certain revelations such as my discovering twenty-two mantis shrimp in the stomach of one respectably-sized striper and of subsequently taking *big* stripers on a fly rod. That story, along with photos, mantis shrimp fly recipes and fishing techniques was first published January 1, 2005 in *Nor'east Saltwater*. Ah, but back to nailing doormat-size fluke.

Carl's secrets of success—apart from his favorite offshore hunting grounds, which doesn't concern us here because I'll be leading you along the primrose shores of Donna's and my own nautical nirvana—are going to be revealed here for two reasons. One reason is that the cat has been let out of the bag (still, many anglers have not adopted it . . . yet). While having served as a member of the board of directors for the New York Sportfishing Federation, I attended a seminar on fluke fishing at the Freeport Recreation Center on Long Island. In one particular session presented by two brothers, Pete and Tom Mikoleski—both highly respected Montauk charter boat captains—I learned that Carl's so-called secret rig was not a secret any longer.

Interestingly, though, several veteran boat captains in the Moriches area, along with a few anglers Carl knows personally and spoke with on the VHF radio during the course of that July 4th holiday, as well as afterward (having compared notes), all having fished the same waters as we had, were nowhere near as productive as our party had been that day. Whereas the three of us, and occasionally Carl's wife, Elizabeth, had caught and released—after limiting out—scores of fat 19- to 24-inch fluke, those other vessels were only averaging two and three fish (not per man) per boat. Intriguing, too, is the fact that not a single one of those old-timers was rigged like Carl and company.

The second reason as to why I'm setting down these words is that I have Carl's permission to do so. Although it's not a so-called secret any longer, few fluke fishermen I see use Carl's deadly lure, limiting themselves to the more traditional approach of using solely a strip of squid and spearing combo. Carl's magic? Well, for starters, a Glow Squid rig with a green glow bead fixed above it, followed by a squid strip/mummichog (killie) combination; more on that setup shortly. Just keep in mind that the lure is deadly when rigged properly. Just how deadly?

Taking you back to Donna's own little corner aboard that 34-foot catamaran, Donna had the first fish, the biggest fish, and unquestionably finished the day heralded as high hook. The fact that Donna was working one rod while Carl had four rods set up along the port rail does not take away from the man's proficiency, for Carl was busy acting as captain and mate from dawn to dusk. He patiently instructed, demonstrated his technique, cut bait, iced down fish, removed half a ton of skate from everyone's rods throughout the course of the day, cleaned up all around us, ran the boat back to those hot spots from where we had drifted, sharpened hooks, and told both funny and poignant stories about fishing the open waters of yesteryear with his father. How did *I* fare, you might ask? My excuse is that in between fishing and conversing, I had taken copious notes so as to retain the knowledge Carl imparted. I came in last, right behind Elizabeth, who for most of that day had tended to two teenagers. However, I did manage to catch my fair share of fish—skates and sea robins mostly, along with a dozen nice 17- to 19-inch (legal size back then) fluke. Not too shabby.

But this is not nearly the end of the story. Donna and I had a chance to work Carl's magic aboard our own boat and in our own waters with our newfound knowledge. Whereas we would occasionally nail a nice fluke here and there in Gardiners Bay and the Greenlawns, now armed with Carl's tackle, tactics and know-how, we easily caught our limit and then some, keeping what we needed for dinner, releasing the rest for another day. They weren't as big as some of those ocean flatties that Donna, Carl and Elizabeth had caught aboard *Finally* that day, yet they were decent size fish; 18 inches on average. Admittedly, the ratio of keepers to throwbacks wasn't nearly the same as when fluke fishing with Captain Schnitter, but it was now late in the season, and many a flattie were bound for the ocean, programmed for the Continental Shelf. Nevertheless, two very satisfied souls returned home from Gardiners and the Greenlawns; nevertheless, having enjoyed unending action through the month of July. We didn't always catch our limit by the time August drew to a close, but we did come home with dinner, stories and pictures for lasting memories. Over the years, the two of us have experimented with various setups in order to satisfy ourselves that it wasn't just one particular bait but rather the squid strip/mummichog (killie)/Glow Squid combination that were working its magic charm.

What to bring besides bait and a boatload of confidence between mid-May into early September? Steve Sekora's Glow Squid Lures, for openers. Find and purchase a few packages in your local tackle store, then go home and fashion your own according to specific requirements recommended by Carl. As promised, we'll cover that procedure step by step. You'll find the bodies and beads you'll need sold separately in most well-stocked tackle shops. Make sure the Glow Squid bodies and beads are the fluorescent type. I had rigged a batch for a new season using fluorocarbon line in lieu of monofilament. It's the way to go as more and more boat captains I speak to are using that line as leader material. It gives the added advantage of virtual invisibility within the water column, so whether you're fishing in crystal clear conditions, the suds or murky waters, you're covered.

An early argument concerning fluorocarbon was that, all things being equal, the product isn't as strong as monofilament (nylon), of which most leader material is made. Yes and no. Don't you just love those kinds of responses? Let's separate fact from fiction. Fluorocarbon, to quote Tom Rosenbauer, author of *The Orvis Streamside Guide to Leaders, Knots, and Tippets*, says, "Unlike nylon, which absorbs up to 30 percent water and gets proportionally weaker, PVDF (polyvinylidenfluoride) does not, so it loses less knot strength than nylon." The downside? Cost. "Fluorocarbon costs about three times as much as nylon," he adds. However, it wouldn't be a rationalization to figure that what you would save by rigging your own lures would certainly offset the cost factor. Besides, we're talking leader lengths measured in feet, not yards upon yards of that material to fill a reel. A spool of fluorocarbon goes a long way. Apply the word amortize to the equation and we're talking cheap insurance. Still unconvinced? Then go up in rated test strength if in doubt, and put your mind at ease. The fact that PVDF is impervious to ultraviolet rays and less susceptible to chemicals and abrasion should be the clincher.

The nice part about rigging your own terminal tackle is that you get to select what you wish. Like the type of hook. There are many on the market. Gamakatsu in Octopus-Red in sizes #1 to 2/0 is a favorite of mine, along with Owner, Mustad, VMC, or Eagle Claw hooks. Not having a hook sharpener close at hand to touch up the point every now and then is tantamount to utilizing a butter knife to cut a tough grade of meat. Why not give yourself the added edge?

The sinkers we used in the ocean that July 4th day ran between 5 to 6 ounces in 42 to 65 feet of water. In and around some areas of Gardiners Bay and the Greenlawns, it was a pleasure to drop that weight down to 2 and 3 ounces on average.

But have those other heftier leads handy if the current and wind are cranking. Bank sinkers painted yellow, which I also used for flounder fishing, work well as attractors.

Glow Squid Rig

In setting up your single Glow Squid rig, you do not *need* a lot of hardware or fancy hi-lo spinner rigs with a multitude of beads. Start with a single 1/0 or 2/0 fluke hook and two fluorescent beads: one set just below the Glow Squid to prevent the lure from working itself down along the shank of the hook, which would thwart the imitation's tentacles from fluttering freely; the other bead set atop the artificial, serving as an attractor. A 40-inch length of 20- to 30-pound test fluorocarbon leader tied to your main line, along with a dropper loop large enough to accommodate different size sinkers (positioned in the middle of the leader) will work well. When you've finished snelling, looping and tying on a barrel swivel, you'll have an approximate 30-inch fluke rig. Perfect. Although Donna and I use hi-lo rigs from time to time (usually to discover what may be patrolling right above that watery floor), we prefer this single hook setup.

Your best bait for fluke, bar none, is fresh squid if you can get it. Not unlike us humans, those flatfish love fresh calamari—hold the sauce. Hitting lighted docks, jetties and harbors with a pink sabiki rig or squid jig during a mid-May evening will produce the desired result. Not unlike the squid themselves, residents of the Greenport area, as well as folks that come from miles around, are drawn like a magnet to such places where squid abound. Railroad Dock is a favorite. Two ½-inch wide tapering strips of squid, approximately 4 inches long—pennant-shaped but with its pointed ends truncated—was our captain's advice. Carl then cuts three-quarters of the way up the middle of each strip in order to create a nice fluttering action in the water column. When threading the strip, avoid creating a crease near the top of the flesh. Nice and flat for those flatfish, I remind myself.

To top off the fresh bait combo, Carl swears by *live* mummichogs (killies), especially the more colorful (black and silver) males. Frozen spearing or sand eels hooked through the eye will, of course, catch fluke, too, but not in greater numbers as with live bait. Therefore, a killie trap is the ticket. Set one from dockside or shoreline with the skeletal remains (frames) of any fish you've cleaned (I keep several frames frozen in plastic zip-lock bags), and you're in business. If there is baitfish in the area, you'll have enough for a day's outing within minutes. Before I had built-in baitwells aboard, I kept the killies alive in a battery-operated Min-O^2-Life Bait Station Cooler with portable aerator; model #1404, manufactured by Frabill. Don't leave home without it. You are now ready for "Flat City."

This livewell is one handy little item for keeping baitfish alive and kicking, especially with limited space aboard a vessel. Compact and easily accessible, the 8-quart, 15 x 7.5 x 8-inch portable bait station (with aerator attached) will prove invaluable. Its outstanding features include a hard shell, double wall, molded-in poly foam insulation that keeps both H_2O and live bait at a constant temperature. Its tight lip around the lid reduces spills. The unit boasts a lift-out net liner, which allows you to quickly secure a baitfish without taking a bath. No time wasted in trying to secure that one particular fat killifish you're after. Lift and promptly pick the winner and be done with it. No need to hunt for that minnow net that you probably misplaced to begin with.

And this you can't help but like a lot: the portable unit includes a built-in night-light for when the moon disappears behind the clouds and your flashlight is either mislaid or on the fritz. Two Duracell D-cell alkaline batteries (not included) power a high-volume diaphragm-drive air pump to ensure an oxygenated environment for approximately eighty hours! Frabill claims that their model 1404 Bait Station cooler "effectively sustains two to three times the volume of bait kept in standard minnow buckets." What I can attest to is the fact that Donna and I have attended very few funerals with an ample supply of live bait in Frabill's cooler. Quite important is its non-kink air hose feature. Bend or twist an ordinary line back upon itself, and kiss that bait good-bye.

As I am admittedly a fusspot, I made a slight modification to the unit. No big deal, really. Considering that the aerator is hung from the cooler via a clip that could easily separate from the unit, I merely ran a cable tie through a notch at the top of the aerator to the station's exterior bracket. This left a one-inch gap between the aerator and the cooler. To fill the space so that the aerator doesn't bounce around, I simply attached a 3.5 x 2 x 1-inch sponge to the cooler via Velcro. *Voilà*! No, that's not French for being anal retentive. Just because the sponge happened to be light yellow to match the cooler lid doesn't make me an ol' fuddy-duddy. Does it? Anyhow, the unit is truly a godsend.

If you wish to tie a deadly bait-lure/fly combo in tandem, try this one on for size. Trail a Lefty's Deceiver (fly) 3 to 4 inches behind a live killie/fresh squid/Glow

Squid offering. I call it my Smorgasbord Rig. Don't miss this trick; the fluke surely do not. You'll have fewer near misses for the simple reason that if the first one doesn't get'em, the second one will.

As a reminder, don't forget a fluke net and charts for your area. Also, have a flashlight handy to shine upon the Glow Squid and beads on days when the sun fails to cooperate. The light that the lure retains (though temporary), down in those murky depths, will pay great dividends. Take along extra batteries as a backup for the flashlight as well as the mini livewell. Bring binoculars, too, and a camera if you're so inclined, for very few folks are going to believe your fish stories in the weeks and months ahead.

Next, pray for a light wind. Donna and I have caught fluke on a doleful zero-knot drift, but were, of course, more productive when the wind picked up a bit; e.g., one to two knots. Conversely, when the current and/or wind god sent our 22-foot pilothouse sailing, we needed to throw out a line tied to a 5-gallon bucket off a stern corner so as to slow us down some. A sea anchor (a.k.a. drift sock), acting as a sort of brake, is a sensible alternative. In any event, when fishing the open waters of Gardiners, I'd advise you to pick your days.

A little history is in order here. Gardiners Island was the first permanent English settlement dating back more than three hundred years. The island is situated between the Twin Forks; that is, the north and south forks of Long Island. It's not at all unusual to spot early morning deer parading the shoreline, or view ospreys flying high above Bambi. For an added treat, have those binoculars handy in addition to that camera.

The Greenlawns, located on the west side of Shelter Island, just north of Jessup Neck, is your best bet from the middle of May through June. But as the waters warm and the action wanes, Donna and I head out to the cooler waters of Gardiners Bay. So pick your area as carefully as you pick your days. And don't forget your foul weather gear just in case NOAA misleads you. They're very much like law enforcement authorities, meaning that they're immune from prosecution when they make serious mistakes.

Location, location, location; or in this case, structure, structure, structure; that's what it's all about. Consult your charts and look for sudden drop-offs and troughs. If you can't pick up a drift along its edge, then cross and be ready for a hookup. If you can run parallel to a sand bar, staying out of harm's way, of course, then do so. Not to have a depth recorder and current navigation charts aboard is asking for trouble. I know a fellow in construction who carries charts dating back to around the time of the Flood, and he wonders why he often runs aground. "It's not like those foundations you pour," I tell him. "Structure can shift from time to time. You know, like those icebergs that you have pictured there on that antiquated chart," I tease, "that floated down from Scandinavia, but have since melted eons ago," I continue. He smiles and tells me he has lots of money. "If that's the case, knock your props off," I retort. "It's a short season for those marine mechanics and salvage guys anyhow." The former of whom should be treated as gods; the latter . . . well, nevermind.

The area in and around Gardiners Island and Shelter Island is magnificent. But you have to see it for yourself in order to appreciate its beauty. If one could write like the French artist Gustave Courbet had painted landscapes and seascapes, one still couldn't do justice to the surrounding splendor. Even the Ruins are aesthetically appealing in some wondrous way. Cruising toward Gardiners Point, you'll see the Ruins. Locate it on your chart and fish the area just to the west, working from 72 through 42 feet of water. If you haven't nailed a keeper, drift down into the twenties; you should score. Fish the Bostwick Bay area, working your way to the other side of the island at Eastern Plain Point, in and around Tobaccolot Bay, covering 22 to 42 feet. It's here that you'll have a good chance of picking up a doormat. Fluke are not the only species you'll find as you're sure to run into some porgies and blues. The weakfish haven't been around in the numbers like they once were, but a boat nearby did pick up a hefty sea trout. Black sea bass and blackfish are in the area, too. They make fine table fare.

If you know that you're going to be fluking in the area prior to the end of June, I'd first give the Greenlawns a shot because those fish simply haven't found it necessary to head east and hit those cooler, deeper holes as yet. You won't find the Greenlawns on the chart; you just have to know and ascribe to local knowledge. Locals call it The Lawns. As mentioned, it's on the west side of Shelter Island. If you're traveling from the east, cruise around Shelter Island from the south side—and for two reasons. One, you can tuck in at Coecles Harbor for a break, or plan on staying overnight. Two, you can continue on to West Neck. If you're staying over, consider the wind and plan accordingly. Wind out of the west, anchor at Coecles; out of the east, anchor at West Neck. Both places are protected and delightful. Consult Dozier's *Waterway Guide* for further information.

In either case, continue around to the west until you see, you guessed it, 'green lawns' off your starboard bow along Shelter Island Sound . . . unless, of course, the lawn guys didn't fertilize this season. I trust it's all organic. Anyhow, you're there! Work the area through 78 feet of water southwest across to Cedar Beach Point opposite Shelter Island, or northwest to Jenning's Point on the Shelter Island side.

Another sound reason as to why I suggested a course along this particular route is to have you encircle this most enchanting island for its splendid scenery and fluking at its finest. Whether you live close by or just visiting the East End of Long Island area, make it a point to get in on the action.

Chapter 13

STRIPED BASS BEWARE

THE OLD BALLOON TRICK ~ ESPECIALLY EFFECTIVE WITH EELS

Plus a Bonus Secret of Sorts

There are so-called fishing secrets that are nothing more than a new spin on time-tested tactics. Then again, there are honest-to-goodness secrets that are passed down from generation to generation of hard-core fishermen—secrets that are kept secure within a circle of old-timers, of which even torture would not elicit a whisper among a single one of them. Lest I be accused of high treason, or something along those lines, I'll take a safer and healthier tact by offering a simple but productive method of nailing big bass and blues. Additionally, I'll conclude this chapter with a bonus secret of sorts. What we'll examine forthwith is a time-honored, test-proven, but often forgotten technique. The Old Balloon Trick was shown to my soul mate and me by an old-timer who came alongside our boat while we were fishing Flanders Bay. The final result was bucket-mouthed bass and tackle-busting blues in the bargain.

The word *bargain* is as good a place to start as any. Your investment will run approximately a dime for a single balloon. You can't beat that. However, I would suggest that you purchase a package of 12-inch, latex, helium-quality (not helium-filled) balloons. A package of fifteen ran Donna a dollar. So, unless you feel the need to actually launch party balloons with personalized inscriptions advertising your event, a plain but durable yellow balloon, sold in most department stores, will do quite nicely. In fact, one lasted me more than a month before it lost some of its flair and air. Additionally, that salty captain who befriended us, offering the item along with instruction, pointed out the merits of employing the color yellow because of its high visibility in low-light conditions, noting that you can easily discern anomalous movement upon the water.

I have an avid bowhunting buddy who occasionally fishes with Donna and me. Once he witnesses this technique, he'll undoubtedly try and hunt down camouflaged patterned balloons—either that or fashion his own. In theory, that may not be a bad idea, as you might want to consider blending in rather than advertising your presence to other fishermen on the water, whether drifting along some quiet backwater or the open bay. Once this often forgotten method of big bobber fishing resurfaces, it could well act as a magnet for the curious. Folks, not fish, are what I'm alluding to. Before you know it, it could look like a wild party out there, with serious vessels in the six-ton class following us little guys for a change of pace, instead of the other way around.

"Forget about eyeballin' those friggin' birds, fellas," might fast become the cry from a salty bay or sea captain of an eighty-plus footer. "Keep your peepers peeled for those telltale bright balloons!"

Humor and—perhaps—hyperbole aside, the color choice is yours. Yellow, however, does work well. No need to go crazy with a set of permanent colored markers as I feel my bowhunting buddy might in an attempt to cloak this neat technique. It's at this point that Donna and I will leave our friend home alone to color by his lonesome. Some folks love to complicate matters. Keeping things simple is the key to having fun and success. Or as former teacher and outdoors writer William (Doc) Muller would say, "Keeping matters simple improves your learning curve." It is a guiding principle that will keep you out of trouble.

At this point, I'm sure you have the picture that employing a balloon as a bobber wasn't, nor isn't, classified information. The amicable captain who approached us and wanted to share his knowledge, handing Donna that yoke-yellow balloon, hardly had a secret under wraps. We, too, share our knowledge—unless we're under oath. In any event, you may see Donna and me working a bright colored balloon somewhere around R"8" off Simmons Point, through the Peconics: Great Peconic Bay, Little Peconic Bay—while heading out east.

Although the balloon bobber may be used in conjunction with your favorite bait, utilizing either a spin or baitcasting outfit, the method is especially advantageous when live lining eels, as the inflated bobber prevents that snakelike creature from burrowing itself backward into the structure's bottom. Too, the balloon signals the perfect moment for when to set the hook. When? When that indicator moves steadily in a given direction and your heart skips a beat as the balloon suddenly picks up momentum would be the answer. Keeping a watchful eye on your depth finder and setting the balloon accordingly to where you want the eel in the water column is crucial. In other words, you wouldn't want twelve feet of line snaking around in three feet of water. Conversely, you wouldn't want three feet of line suspended in a twelve-foot column if you suspect the fish you are targeting are feeding near the bottom.

Attaching the knotted part of the inflated balloon onto slick monofilament and have it stay in place can be tricky, as it will tend to slide. Experiencing this problem, I looped the line through the eye of a snap swivel (as you would a sinker) so that I could run the swivel up or down where needed. Next, I simply attached the snap between the neck of the balloon and the knotted seal, locking it in place. It works well.

As I promised you a bonus secret of sorts, I'll conclude this chapter with the following anecdote:

Friends and acquaintances that Donna and I have made through our outdoor adventures are priceless. As I'm primarily an award-winning novelist with five published thrillers and seven more in manuscript form, along with scores of articles and editorials to my credit, I occasionally meet other writers. One such writer wrote a weekly column encompassing the great outdoors. As most of my novels include outdoor adventures, this fellow and I struck up a rapport. We shared several *secrets* with regard to both hunting and fishing. Mine went to the grave with the gentleman some years ago, for he had suddenly died of a massive heart attack at age fifty. Certain secrets, along with his writings—of which I considered him to be among the very best in his field—will remain with me to the end. His name was . . . (I still have trouble using the past tense here) Wayne Nester. His wife, Pamela Greene, a former council member for the Town of Islip, accompanied Wayne and participated in many an outdoor hunting and fishing adventure. Wayne and Pam reminded Donna and me of ourselves. That is, couples who share a love of the great outdoors. I was to help Wayne with a novel; he was to help me break into writing outdoor articles, as most of my editorials and other writings had concerned the criminal justice system at the time. Neither of us got the chance to work together, for he died shortly after we met. Among the secrets Wayne shared with me, one I know he wouldn't mind my sharing with you now, is: "Don't tell anyone that the great outdoors is as close as many folks are ever going to get to God; otherwise, we're going to be overrun," he had added with a mischievous gleam in his eye as he sent a streamer fly to the far side of an expansive canal in back of the couple's home. I believe that the great outdoors serves as a sort of church for many of us.

That very fall, shortly after Wayne passed away, I released one special helium-filled balloon heavenward as a symbolic gesture to my friend. Not thirty seconds later, I hooked into and landed a nice size striper using The Old Balloon Trick. Perhaps Wayne did help me out after all because the contents discovered in the stomach of that linesider held twenty-two mantis shrimp, which led to my first in a series of fly-fishing articles.

With regard to this chapter, please do not judge me too harshly if you find yourself navigating your craft through a vast sea of many colored balloons in the coming seasons.

Chapter 14

BLUEFISH BONANZA

Donna with a 29-inch bluefish

Up from the southern waters and along the continental shelf came those choppers to keep Donna and me busy during late April and into early May. The blues had been skinny by comparison to the imminent fall run, their spawning ordeal now behind them as they fattened up after ravaging every sound, bay, estuary and inlet along a northerly path. Those cannibalistic creatures were soon to create havoc anew in our area for a spell, mixed in among stripers and fluke, with the month of October reaching the pinnacle of mayhem. Where exactly? Everywhere—from Orient and Montauk to the New York Bight and beyond. Of course, there were those listless days of summer when nothing took the hook but the heat. But come September, gather your wits about you and get ready for some serious action targeting (it's hard not to hit the bull's-eye) those gorillas on parade.

Decades ago, I introduced a good friend of mine to fishing a body of water back in Bayville, near the bridge. Along with Richie Roberts came my five-year-old son that early morning, as Jason had accompanied me on many a fishing trip, mostly for flounder back in those good old days. On the drive out from Bayside, Richie had asked numerous questions about the fish we were targeting. Even though I was pretty new at the game, having fished predominately fresh water, I answered all his questions with authority, for I had quickly learned that there were few wrong answers when it came to tangling with those ubiquitous blues, from the type of bait and equipment employed, right down to the fishing knots applied.

At an early age, Jason could tie two knots rather efficiently, in addition to the laces of his shoes. The clinch knot was his favorite. He tied practically everything with that knot back then, including painters (bowlines) fastened to pilings for our little boat. With his very own flounder/snapper rod, he'd tie line to leader and hook, executing a dropper loop for 1½- to 2-ounce sinker set a foot or so above the bait. The bait? Anything that swam or crawled in the water: bloodworms, sandworms, clams, spearing, sand eels and crabs. You couldn't go wrong. That morning, however, Jason's ultra-light rod was purposely left back in Bayside.

I had arranged for the three of us to start out *early* to catch the tide, heading for the bait shop where I kept the boat. It was still dark.

"And what tide might that be?" Richie asked with mild but apparent irritation, short on sleep and long on questions.

"Either side of the top of the tide; it doesn't much matter," I answered up confidently, noting that the store was still closed when we arrived. No problem, for I was fully prepared.

"If it doesn't much matter, then what are we doing here so *early*? It's still pitch black!" Richie complained.

"Early bird gets the worm."

"I thought we were after fish."

"Hand me that flashlight and the tackle box." I opened the box while Richie suggested that we find an open coffee shop so as to kill time until first light.

"They're not open at this hour, Richie," I stated with a smile he certainly could not see. Tell him, J."

Jason just yawned and nodded in the affirmative.

"Besides, I have everything we need right here in this box. Believe me," I said encouragingly, holding up a plug practically the length of the beam of light.

"What's that?" Richie gaped.

"An Atom."

"And that's supposed to catch . . . what exactly?"

"You'll soon see."

After we set up the rods and reels and launched my 14-foot Scars fiberglass boat from the beach, I once again explained to Richie that we were targeting blues. Big blues.

"How big?" Richie wanted to know, huddled there in the bow of the boat. "Because that's one hell of a big plug, Bob! And why so many hooks hanging from it?"

"So that from whatever direction they attack — Look!" Headlights lit the shack. A moment later the owner walked up to the front door. "The guy's opening up the store." We picked up bait in the bargain.

As I rigged the rod and Richie held the flashlight, Jason had not taken his eyes off the large silhouetted lure, never-ever having seen his father fish with such a prodigious plug before. "Aren't we going for the same fish we usually go for, Dad?"

"Well, yes. But only bigger."

"Big snappers?"

"Well, the snappers grow into what we call cocktails, usually two to five pounds. After that we call them choppers, alligators, gorillas or monsters."

Jason's eyes widened and his jaw dropped, so I thought it best to put away the intimidating artificial; after all, we now had fresh bait.

When we were finally settled on the water, Richie continued with his endless list of questions.

"Why wire at the end of the line, and what's an Albright anyhow?"

"Bluefish teeth are very sharp," I explained. "That's why they call them tackle busters. As a matter of fact, when we hook into one, and you bring him aboard, I'll take him off the hook because if you're not careful, he could take your finger down to the bone."

I went on to explain the time I was on a party boat when a fellow hauled a brute of a blue over the starboard rail with such force that the fish hit and bit a bare-chested man who was fishing on the port side of the vessel. I was so involved in telling Richie the story, I didn't realize the effect it had on Jason.

Later that morning, at the first sign of light on the horizon, with hope waning by the minute, I was bragging to my friend what a great little fisherman my son is and how he simply loves to be out on the water. But all Jason wanted to know was— "Are we out of bait yet, Dad?" My son kept asking that same question over and over. Of course, Richie just roared with laughter, reassuring Jason that we probably wouldn't catch a thing, but if we did, and it happened to be a *monster* blue, he'd cut the line himself, my good friend swore.

We truly had a nice time out on the calm water but caught not a single fish. Not even a sign of a tern or gull or gannet diving or even circling in the distance could be observed; that is, when daybreak had gradually appeared and you could, indeed, see clearly.

I learned a lot since then. I learned that even the so-called omnipresent bluefish are not always in attendance when and where they should be. I learned to chunk and ladle out some chum on those days when the fish would not cooperate. Ah, but not too much bunker chum because you didn't want to create a slick in back of the boat that leaves a trail across the Sound to Connecticut!

Too, I learned to rig properly by tying my own hi-lo arrangement from a four-foot section of fluorocarbon leader material, double the test strength of the main line; bank sinker on the bottom; one foot up a dropper loop with a 2/0 to 6/0 beak baitholder or sproat hook; another foot up, a second hook suspended by a cork float. I learned how to troll with umbrella rigs, to bucktail and jig a deadly diamond lure, the latter of which we'll examine in a moment. I learned from experience, not hearsay, to keep those popper plugs in abeyance for the fall, for in the springtime those blues are not pursuing larger baits like the humongous Atoms and Creek Chubs I carried in my tackle box. During the spring run, bunker chunks will do just nicely. Fresh bunker is even better if you can get it. Herring and mackerel are favorites also. I determined through trial and error that a falling tide is better than the flood. I discovered early on that few fish, pound for pound, fight like a blue.

Just as importantly, because I love eating fish, I soon learned that big bluefish prepared properly are absolutely delicious (contrary to what some folks claim) and that preparation doesn't begin in the kitchen. It begins the moment you bring a beauty over the gunnel. You want to bleed the fish immediately by running a sharp blade behind its head, down to the bone. Next, you want to gut the fish, remove its gills, wash the flesh in salt water then pack it in ice. When filleting the really big boys, I remove the dark section of meat along the lateral line. That is the secret to bringing a truly big, fresh bluefish from the cutting board to the table. That said, let's examine a few particulars that will up your score in catching these choppers.

One of the most productive methods of nailing blues is jigging, for diamonds are deadly in the depths. Donna and I use them in the fall out at Jessup Neck, around buoy "17" in Little Peconic Bay. Jigging is work, meaning that you're dropping lure and line then reeling up constantly. However, that effort is most mystically transformed into a labor of love the moment a chopper strikes. But like anything else, there is a definite technique. I used to think—you see—that was my problem. I did *too* much thinking and not enough research. Read, try different methods and techniques, evaluate for yourself—*then* don't be afraid to be creative. The fact that you're still with me, reading this chapter, is terrific. And because you are, I'm going to share another little secret: For every medical doctor that <u>pre</u>scribes something, be it medication or just plain advice, there's another doctor out there that will <u>pro</u>scribe (prohibit) what the first professional professed. What to do? Go with the guy or gal in which you have the most confidence. I think it's a lot like fishing. Anyhow, Oscar Wilde said it best: "The only thing to do with good advice is to pass it on." Find your own niche and comfort zone.

Diamond jigs—such as Steve Sekora's types—tubes or plain, simulate baitfish such as spearing and especially sand eels. A 2- to 4-ounce diamond will suffice as I like to stay with light equipment. Someone else might suggest a heftier lure along with a medium to heavy-action rod, especially in deep waters. They're right—for them. See what I mean? Use what works well for you. Ideally, but not practically, we could carry aboard three different rod weights (light, medium, heavy) each fashioning two basic type reels; that is, bait casting and spin casting, which means we're already up to six rods. If we start adding wire or leadcore to the conventional outfits, in addition to monofilament and braided lines to the mix, we could wind up with as many as eighteen setups! Actually, I have an acquaintance who carries five conventional rod and reel setups at all times in addition to four spinning outfits. If he were a fly-fisherman to boot, well, he'd need a bigger boat. Hence, we'll resort back to the power of KISS, instead. Keep It Simple System. If Donna and I were plying the waters well-offshore, that might be another story, meaning heavier outfits. Yet, even that approach is changing in that Shimano—manufacturers of world-famous, fine quality fishing equipment—has recently designed lightweight <u>systems</u> that replace heavy-duty broomstick-like rods, big reels, heavy lines, lengthy lures, weighty sinkers and even bait! These are the items of yesteryear. Shimano's state-of-the-art systems include their Butterfly, Lucanus, Waxwing and Orca lures. Further information is online at fishshimano.com; however, I'll be covering these systems in subsequent chapters.

Remember, broomsticks are strictly for sweeping. Depending on the Shimano System one chooses will determine a rod, reel, line and lure choices. It can get a wee bit complicated. So, once again, keeping that KISS principle firmly in mind, I'll recommend that you jig with a high-speed reel such as a 6.0:1 gear ratio spooled with 20- to 30-pound PowerPro braided line.

If you are happy with your own equipment, not wishing to spend a small fortune on Shimano's state-of-the-art jigging and other systems, believe me, I understand. Keep in mind that if and when you are ready to upgrade, I recommend Shimano's high-end quality products, as you get what you pay for. Even though many companies produce rods and reels to fit every budget, stay on top of your game with top-of-the-line equipment.

So, here we go. Using thumb pressure so as not to create a bird's nest (backlash), release your favorite jig into 27 to 70 feet of water in that riptide around Jessup Neck. You may even get a hit on the way down to Davey Jones' Locker. If not, after the jig hits the bottom and rests for a split second, reel back up five times. Why not four or six? Because I said so, and because five works for me. I know, silly answer. So come up with your own silly formula, but come up steadily. Back down again. Do this constantly until you're tired, then dead-stick the rod and grab a bite of sandwich, and low and behold, that's precisely when your fishing partner will positively get a strike. I guarantee it!

Tired of jigging or being upstaged? Try casting a surface plug along the edge of the pod of baitfish thrashing over your right shoulder. You just know those cannibals are underneath them. Here come the birds to feast upon the spoils of flesh as you hook into a chopper on your first cast. And now Donna has put away her diamond and is throwing out a pencil-thin lure that swims just beneath the surface. Bam! Five minutes later, on a light spinning outfit, a *big* blue is in the boat. Why is her fish three pounds or so bigger than mine? Aren't they supposed to run in schools according to size? And why are those other birds just sitting out *there* in the distance? Waiting. Suddenly the water starts to bubble before it begins to boil then erupts like a miniature volcano. Why are we still *here*? For the action has suddenly stopped. Ah, you don't even have to start the engine because we are drifting toward the madding scene.

The surface and sub-surface plugs are no longer producing. I tie on a 2-ounce Kastmaster and send the deep-diving lure along the periphery of the pod, not in its center. It's bad enough that the bowrider racing towards us might divide the pack and spook the lot. I wave him off and he waves back like he's my best friend. He actually casts into the middle of the mass while his boat is doing fifteen knots. I truly believe his soul mate that is driving is looking for the brakes. The action was over before it really began. It was our fault in part for heading out at noontime on a Labor Day weekend. But all was not lost.

On the way home, Donna spotted a swirl and ordered her captain to approach a pocket of water to the southeast side of the 105 Bridge in the Peconic River. Three casts with the Kastmaster, and she was into something quite respectable. Ten minutes later, she started to hand me the rod.

"Oh, no," I declared. "That's your fish."

"I can't do this anymore."

"Wanna bet?"

"Please," she pleaded.

The fish ran and zigged and zagged and dove. Donna was barely gaining any line. Another five minutes passed.

"I'm exhausted," Donna whined.

"Just imagine how the fish feels," I offered in solace.

"The fish is fine; I'm not gaining any line."

"You're a poet, dear."

A string of profanity negated the compliment.

"You're doing just fine. Don't horse him. He's a brute. "

"You're a brute for making me do this."

"He's practically at the boat. Relax."

"Funny man."

I had the net ready. The fish dove several more times. Another five minutes passed before we took him aboard: a 34½-inch, 14-pound blue on 12-pound test mono line. Another lesson learned, luckily not the hard way, because that line was nicked and frayed, which reduces its strength considerably—probably by more than half. I cut the damaged section off, passed a sharpening stone along the edges of the point of the hook, and we were back in business. I often rig with a plastic coated wire leader such as Serflon when specifically targeting big blues; otherwise, I'll use braid, monofilament or fluorocarbon line tied directly to a barrel swivel connected to a Power/Fast Clip (manufactured by Tactical Anglers) for virtually all our leaders and lures. The owner is "Crazy" Alberto Knie, consummate striped bass fisherman. These clips come in three different sizes and positively belong in your tackle bag or box. I've had conventional name-brand clips open up on a few tackle busters, but never with a Power/Fast Clip.

Donna's fish fed twelve for dinner that evening. I can't get three people together to agree on a time and a place to hit a local restaurant. But fresh filleted or poached bluefish, with even last minute notice, on one of the busiest holidays of the year . . . no problem. Of course, Richie relates Jason's "Are we out of bait yet?" story to everyone present for the umpteenth time, which is why I'll try and nip this in the bud right here and now. If you ever bump into him, you can simply say, "Richie, I heard and read it all before."

Chapter 15

PECONIC PORGIES

Generally speaking, serious anglers of the brine think big, not only in terms of size but also in terms of what is ever-popular. There is no question that stripers, fluke, weakfish, blues, blackfish and black sea bass come immediately to mind when saltwater fishing folks name their favorite six found in Long Island waters. As flounder are not as prolific as they once were, they are not on the tip of everyone's tongue like in days of old when you could easily catch thirty-plus fish per man on a good day. Of course, I'm dating myself, but that's the way it was back then. A rental skiff, a bushel of clams shared among four guys (not necessarily for bait but for slurping down on the half shell on those back bays along with a favorite beverage that begins with the letter B), a couple dozen blood or sandworms (for they were affordable back then), several cans of corn for chumming, light tackle, and you were good to go. Go where? Practically anywhere. The flounder were there. Fat and feisty. "Those good ol' days are pretty much gone forever," old salts will tell you with a tear or two gleaming in the corner of an eye. If you had a mind to take a kid fishing when the weather warmed up a bit, wanting to guarantee the child some action, well, snapper fishing was a sure bet. Snappers certainly are, indeed, a good choice when introducing a youngster to fishing. But if you want the assurance of success coupled with the promise of sheer excitement for children from six to sixty, porgies are the name of the game. They fight like the devil, and the fillets are an added treat. They are truly delicious. As a rule, the further east you travel, the larger the scup. In the Peconics, porgy fishing is at its finest. It can save the day when those other favorites fail to cooperate.

Porgies usually arrive in our waters several weeks before we're allowed to legally take them, so my soul mate and I do not specifically target them until such time that regulations permit. The season seemingly runs helter-skelter, with the New York Marine Recreational Fisheries regulating opened and closed seasons throughout the year, and with good reason. This doesn't mean that you can't introduce a kid to some early action and at the same time teach him or her catch-and-release conservation. Generally, you have about five in-season months in which to have a ball. 2008 through 2012 were exceptionally good years to fish for scup; plentiful and big. Regulations, as with any marine fishery, are subject to change, so always check the current status before venturing out.

Donna and I usually have about four porgy fish-fries a season, inviting family, friends, neighbors and new guests over for a treat. A dialogue will usually ensue somewhere along these lines:

"What's that? What are we having?" several regulars will inevitably ask as I take the lightly breaded morsels from Donna's hands. I try and avoid the question simply because most folks, understandably, form a negative mind-set when entering unfamiliar territory, especially when it comes to food.

If they persist, I'll tell them, "C.O.D."

"Oh, cod?" they may query.

"**C**atch **O**f the **D**ay," I'll reply.

"Which is what?" they'll persist, pushing me into that proverbial corner.

I won't lie, but I will try and stand firm. "Have you ever had a bad meal here?" I'll ask testily.

"Why, I should say not," or words to that effect would unquestionably be their defensive reply.

"Then why should this day be different than any other?"

"So then why can't you just tell us what you're making?"

"Fish fillets," I'll fence.

"I can see that they're fish fillets, Bob. Kind of small, though. All we're asking is what kind of fish fillets?"

"Scup, Skip."

"Ah, scup!" Skip replies, too confounded to take the conversation to the next level, feeling that he should know what scup are, where they hail from, along with how many calories per serving each fillet contains.

"Why don't you make Michelle and yourself a drink, Skippy? The pan's hot and scup take but a second. "

"Good idea."

By the end of the meal, after requesting seconds and even third helpings, everyone knew that they had been eating porgies, all agreeing that they are, indeed, a delicious fish.

"I always heard they were bony," Michelle declares.

"They are," Donna said with a smile. "That's why Bob fillets them.

Admittedly, it's a bit of work but well worth the effort because those medallions are worth their weight in gold. Yes?"

"I never would have believed it," Skip declares.

"It's one of our favorite fishes," I remark.

Every person concurred except one individual: my son. He hasn't eaten fin or shellfish since he was seven years of age. I had him tested, evaluated then retested. He is definitely of sound mind and body; DNA typing clearly confirms that he is, indeed, mine. In defense of his aversion to anything that swims throughout the food chain, Jason will inform guests that he was traumatized as a child, whereby Donna, Jason and I caught many, many freshwater perch while vacationing in the Adirondacks. I practiced conservation then as I do now, inculcating such lessons as, "You take from the waters only what you wish to eat." Is it my fault that our family had fresh fish three times a day for a solid week? There was an occasional largemouth bass or pike thrown into the mix. It's not like they were *all* perch. Donna and I still eat and love fish. Anyhow, Jason still enjoys fishing with his dad when he visits. The fact that I just alluded to myself in the third person does not mean I question the validity of those tests.

Several guests wanted to hear all about porgy fishing. Skip and Michelle only wanted to know when we were having scup again.

"When you come with us and catch a batch of your own," I reply in answer to Skip's question. "And that's the easy part," I tell him candidly. "But then you have to help me clean the boat, the equipment, as well as fillet some of those fish when we get back to the dock. Michelle can assist Donna in the kitchen preparing those delectable delights for the pan. Actually, first time out is a free ride. After that, no free lunch; everybody pitches in. What do you think? Are you up for it sometime?" Before Skip and Michelle could even answer, I had two other couples take me up on my offer.

Porgy fishing is a great outing, particularly for those who have never been fishing or climbed aboard a boat before. As a matter of fact, we convert new folks to our bays and estuaries every year. One wife even *made* her husband buy a boat at the New York Boat Show. Two of my next-door neighbors' nieces, Hannah and Lucy, returned to England with fish-food stories rivaling Dover sole.

Two great spots Donna and I frequent are situated in Little Peconic Bay. One is found along the northwest corner of Robin's Island, around buoy R"4" in 17 to 25 feet of water. The other is in the area of Roger's Rock, southwest of Robin's, around buoys R"28" and R"30" in 22 to 32 feet. Both 'fingers' grace the North and South Race respectively. Consult your chart. Light tackle, a chum pot and some bait are a few of the items you'll need to bring home your limit in a matter of a couple of hours when the fishing is hot. But that's only if you're feeding a hungry family and friends three fish meals a day for a solid week. Hyperbole aside, four nice size porgy fillets feed Donna and me perfectly. There are times that we scale, gut and place two whole porgies within a fish rack set upon our barbecue grill. We love fresh fish as I'm sure you do (our darling Jason being the sole exception). Take what you need for a meal or two, and leave the rest for another day. In past years, the bag limit was fifty scup per person.

"Fifty porgies!" I'd repeatedly exclaim to Donna across the span of seasons. "When is the fisheries management going to wake up?" I had complained one summer in particular. "And what *ever* in the world is that family over there going to do with that five-gallon bucket filled with porgies?" I whispered when we pulled up to a dock.

"Traumatize their children like you surely did to Jason," was my mate's response.

But seriously, I had to know. I didn't have to wait long for an answer, for their eldest child questioned the mother, wondering if they really had enough fish for their garden.

"Did you hear that?" I hissed in exasperation. "Fertilizer!"

"Zip it up," was the boss' comment as she was now on terra firma and I was no longer the captain in command.

"But—"

"Quiet!"

When bottom fishing these inshore waters for porgies, I prefer a light baitcasting outfit. Adhering to the principle of KISS, **K**eep **I**t **S**imple **S**ystem, a pair of five-and-a-half foot graphite Ugly Sticks coupled to our Penn 930 Levelmatics, spooled with 20-pound test braided line are the ticket for Donna and me. This doesn't mean you run out and buy that particular rod and hard-to-get reel. I'm only suggesting that you fish for scup with a light-action outfit, for you're not going to have nearly as much fun using a broomstick (very heavy-action rod).

For your terminal tackle, you can simply purchase a few packages of either single leader or pre-rigged high-lo porgy hooks then learn to tie your own. A #4 sproat or beak bait-saver hook is a good choice. Construct the rig from a 24-inch section of 20-pound test fluorocarbon with a 4-inch dropper loop tied in the middle to accommodate 1- 1½- 2- or 3-ounce sinkers, which should suffice. Fluorocarbon gives you the added edge because it is virtually invisible in the water column. Additionally, fluorocarbon has less stretch (which translates into better sensitivity), is more abrasion resistance than monofilament, and is impervious to ultraviolet light.

It is essential that you learn at least three basic knots when rigging terminal tackle or simply tying a hook or leader to your line: a clinch knot, a dropper loop, and a surgeon's loop. These knots are demonstrated step-by-step on line or can be found in handouts on the counter in tackle shops. Too, if the shopkeeper isn't busy, don't be afraid to ask him or her to show you a couple of knots. Make it your business to learn a knot a month, practice them, and you'll soon be teaching others. I first practice with a HI-VIS braided mono running line until I get the hang of it before switching over to clear monofilament or fluorocarbon. It makes things so much easier. Later on, you may want to purchase one of several knot books on the market.

An assortment of bait may be used on those silvery thieves. Soft baits will tend to frustrate as those fish are fast and devious pilferers. The tougher peripheral strips of chowder or skimmer clams threaded on bait-saver (bait-holder) hooks, mentioned above, are excellent and will help the situation considerably. In any event, use only small pieces of clam or squid. Sand or bloodworms (about the size of a thumbnail) are excellent baits, too, although costly and, I feel, unnecessary.

Note that a chum pot can make or break a day. It is absolutely essential. A couple of logs of clam chum and you can practically guarantee success, provided, of course, that porgies are in the area. You'll be anchored, not drifting (unless you want to lose a couple of rigs in a single pass) because the structures you need to search for are shell beds and rocky bottoms. When locating such structure, avoid the hub of the city; anchor your boat along its outskirts, setting up a nice slick. Trash fish such as cunners (bergalls) will remain above the bed while your porgy prizes will follow their noses. Work up-tide of that structure and you are sure to score. Search out boulders and where sandy and stony bottoms meet. That is porgy haven; you'll be in angler's heaven. Engage your reel and be ready. Check that drag. No slack in that line, Jack. When you feel a tap-tap-tap, just set the hook by lifting, then steadily reel, reel, reel.

If you haven't guessed by now, you'll need and should have a depth recorder aboard for a couple of reasons: first, to locate desirable structure for those fish you're targeting; secondly, to stay out of harm's way. It is a most valuable piece of equipment.

For the most part, you make your own luck in this world. Nevertheless, good luck and tight lines to you, followed by great meals because porgies are hard to beat when it comes to fine fare.

"Right, Skip?"

"Right, Bob. Listen, you were going to show me how to tie a worm knot, remember?"

"Righhht."

Chapter 16

BLACKFISH

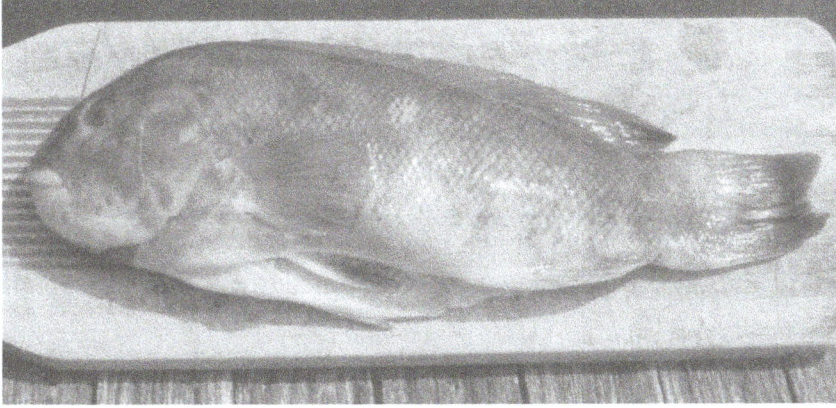

Though not the prettiest fish in the sea, blackfish are, without question, among the tastiest fare you will find. Therefore, Donna and I take the time to seek them out in anticipation of a fine meal. Like all fishing, learn to recognize their local habitat in relationship to meal preference, and you'll score handsomely. In realizing this, we study our charts carefully and pay strict attention to our depth sounder/fish-finder unit. Like any good piece of real estate, it's all about location, location, location. Apply that adage to angling, and you'll quickly learn that it's all about structure, structure, structure.

And what structure might that be? Rock-strewn areas ranging from stone-sized rubble to prodigious boulders are where you will find blackfish, commonly called tautog or white chins. Blackfish are bottom feeders. Explore rocky areas in fairly deep inshore waters, and you are off to a good start. If you can locate oyster beds or areas where mussels abound, you will do well. Too, you will have little trouble discovering territory where barnacles teem. "Barnacles?" you may be tempted to question. Yes, those tiny but troublesome marine creatures that attach themselves to your prop and outdrive; those prolific aquatic crustaceans that adhere themselves in great numbers to the bottom of your boat if you fail to take the necessary precautions with primers and paints. Ah, but in those very areas where barnacles abound lie territories that will hold blackfish like a magnet. Think jetties, bridge abutments, pilings, docks, piers, rock piles and reefs. Yes, barnacles—those delectable morsels upon which white chins feed in addition to other saltwater shell life. Blackfish have the dental work to deal with these tenacious forms. Offer tautog a selection of their favorite foods such as small crabs, and you are sure to score nicely; more on that subject in a moment.

From October 5th through December 14th, 2013, the New York State Department of Environmental Conservation permits us to pursue these robust fighters. Toward the end of yet another season on the water (a fortnight before the close of striped bass fishing on December 31st), Donna and I don our Gor-Tex/Thinsulate clothing and footwear, heading out for the finale. We leave behind light tackle and wield medium to medium-heavy artillery, which is needed not necessarily to hook but to lift and pull these denizens from the deep. Rest assured that they are not far from a fissure that will play havoc with hook, line and sinker—a crevice that will claim your terminal tackle quicker than you can say, "Son of a salty #^*$%^#*! Believe me. Donna has a set choice of expletives that she never quite gets to complete before her rig is securely caught between . . . well, a rock and a hard place. As for myself, let's just say that I understand the frustration that one experiences when a person decides to take out his wrath on a golf club that didn't quite meet his or her expectations. Resign yourself to the fact that you are going to lose some equipment, save the rod and reel, so long as you don't hurl them into the drink. Blackfish are notorious thieves; they will persistently steal you bait. What to do?

There are different schools of thought on when and how to set the hook; that is, immediately or momentarily—lightly or with vigor? Arbitrarily deciding which method to employ is silly, for there are important variables to consider, such as whether you are spooled with monofilament or braided line. Braided line translates to sensitivity, and it is sensitivity that is needed to help you distinguish between a tap and a tug. Allow blackfish to tap. Set the hook solidly on a tug, lifting and reeling that critter off the bottom before it has a chance to delve into a cave-like chamber.

In addition to the inshore areas mentioned above, fishing over wrecks in far deeper waters of Long Island Sound may require 12-ounce sinkers or larger, depending on currents and wind. There will be some days when fishing for blackfish around Orient or Orient Point that you'll need 20 ounces to hold bottom. But for most inshore action, depending on location, 2 to 6 ounces of lead will get the job done. My advice is that you would be wise to carry not only a wide range of sinkers to cover a given situation, but a good many because you are certain to need replacements. Locate big boulders on a chart, and you are probably on blackfish real estate.

Although many anglers use conventional reels and rods for blackfish, Donna and I prefer spinning reels married to rods with some backbone, yet with a flexible enough tip to feel those taps and tugs. Broomsticks (very heavy-action rods) have their application but at the cost of sheer feel, fight and overall fun. A Shakespeare SP 1101 6-foot 6-inch Medium-Heavy Action spinning rod, or a Shakespeare SP 1100 6-foot Heavy Action stick, both under the label Ugly Stik, are two excellent rods with enough backbone and surprising flexibility to tackle tautog in the 10-pound class. Matched to a Shimano Sustain 5000 FG or Stradic 5000 FJ spinning reel, both with a 6.2:1 gear ratio in order to swiftly lift those brutes off the bottom, you are now ready for serious action whether in 15, 50, or 100 feet of water. For our inshore fishing, Donna and I spool with 30-pound test PowerPro braided line. Remember, 30-pound braid is the equivalent diameter of 8-pound test monofilament. That gives you some serious sensitivity as well as greater line capacity.

In rigging terminal tackle for blackfish action, tie the main line (braid) to one end of a barrel swivel (rated for 50-pound test) then employ a uni-knot. With a 3-foot length of 20- to 25-pound test monofilament or fluorocarbon, tie the leader material to the other end of a barrel swivel by employing an improved clinch knot. At the bottom of the leader, make a wide enough loop to accommodate a wide range of bank sinkers (2 to 20 ounces); tie off the loop by employing a double surgeon's knot. Make a 3- to 4-inch dropper loop a foot above the sinker to accommodate the hook.

Note that not all barrel swivels and other hardware are created equal. You get what you pay for. Stick with marine-grade hardware such as Sea Striker or Rosco.

When I first got hooked on blackfishing, I quickly learned that a good hook was crucial to the game. Cheap hooks will cheat you as will the wrong size and style hook. A #6 hook is a good middle-of-the-road size, easily handling 6- to 8-pound fish, which is what you can encounter in our bays as well as Long Island Sound. Candidly, most of the blackfish we nail are in the 3 to 4 pound class, and a #8 hook would be fine. When heading out to the wrecks, dealing with deep water and double-digit denizens, consider 2/0 or 3/0 Pro-Series Gamagatsu Octopus hooks.

Now, back to bait. Blackfish love crabs, and hermit crabs rank among the best bait. Hermit crabs are not a single particular crab but rather pertain to a number of crabs of the genera Pagurus and Eupagurus. Listed below are the white chins' favorites, along with their commonly referred to regional names closed within parenthesis. You will note that some of the names overlap. An indispensable guidebook to identification is Alan Caolo's *Fly Fisherman's Guide to Atlantic Baitfish & Other Food Sources*. The title is a misnomer in that it is truly a practical handbook for anglers—inclusive of spin and bait casting. This book absolutely belongs in your personal library. It contains fantastic photographs of Atlantic rock crabs, (stone crab, red crab); lady crabs (calico crab, sand crab, swimming crab); blue crabs (blue claw, blue shell); fiddler crabs (fiddlers); mole crabs (sand flea, sand crab, sand bug); mud crabs (stone crab, rock crab); green crabs (shore crab). Green crabs are blackfishes' favored mollusks, although difficult for us to come by. Fiddlers are the more popular choice in that they are easily accessible.

Again, blackfish have powerful teeth to crack, crush then suck in those fleshy morsels. Not to be overlooked in their food chain are skimmer clams and mussels; grass shrimp (sand shrimp, shrimp, prawn); blood and sand worms; even spearing. These softer baits are surely delicacies that require little effort on the part of blackfish to gobble down greedily. The ticket to success is live bait. We keep ours fresh in a livewell.

Crabs such as fiddlers should be baited by removing one of its claws and inserting the hook into that opening, working it in and around so that the point is hidden but faces fractionally forward of its interior edge, smack between its eyes. Discipline yourself to resist taps as the target first takes and cracks the crab's shell. Only when you feel the tug do you set the hook hard, lift and reel steadily. Once again, these fish are fast and will steal your bait more often than not. It takes a bit of getting used to, to play their game and come out the winner. Practice does *not* necessarily make perfect; herein lies the challenge. Bring plenty of bait and terminal tackle. After a while, you'll get the hang of hooking and hauling up these tough fighters. In a word—fun.

Whereas striped bass fishing is generally more productive at night, togs are chiefly a daytime deal. The time of day that frequently moves blackfish into action is the final hour before sunset—right up until the moment before dark. It's like the group decided on the last sitting for their evening meal. Donna and I find this setting more dependable than concerning ourselves with facets of a tide. Keeping a detailed log through the years will aid you in making important determinations whether fishing for tautog or tuna.

Chapter 17

BLACK SEA BASS

Ron Atkinson with a 24½ inch black sea bass

Generally speaking, a good many recreational anglers catch black sea bass (a.k.a. sea biscuits or knobs-heads) as a by-product of the fish they are actually targeting—particularly fluke, blackfish and porgies. During 2009–2012, big blowfish had come across the rail with sea bass as well. Of course, there are recreational fishermen who specifically target sea bass and have enjoyed doing so year-round as was the case during an uninterrupted period between 2006 through 2009. Prior to 2006, sea bass sharpies had to contend with both split and limited seasons, with the exception of 2002 when anglers enjoyed a year-round season. For 2010, however,

New York State Marine Regulations limited our season for sea bass from May 22nd until September 12th. Minimum size was 12½ inches. You were allowed 25 sea bass a day. What's wrong with this picture? Personally, I would like to see an "open-all-year" season, but with the number of fish permitted drastically reduced. Several sea bass per recreational angler should surely suffice; four folks on a privately-owned fishing vessel do not need nor should be allowed to take a hundred black sea bass. Party boats and private charters are a different story. For 2012, our sea bass season was to end December 31st, not open again until June 15th, 2013; 13-inch minimum size; 15 fish per angler. However, regulations can change in a heartbeat, and it did. The New York State Department of Conservation extended the season to run to February 28th, 2013; 12½-inch minimum size; 15 fish per angler. The point of all this is that you have to be on top of your game concerning marine regulations.

In any event, why do some anglers set their sights on sea bass? The answer is that they are one of the finest tasting fish from our waters. Some would argue that they are *the* absolute best. I rank sea bass right up there with winter flounder and those medallions of porgies mentioned earlier. Now, that's saying something!

Specifically targeting sea bass is not difficult. Hum. The words 'not difficult' somehow subliminally connote yet a degree of difficulty, so allow me to rephrase. Targeting sea bass is, in fact, downright easy. What may be considered difficult is catching *large* sea bass, but we'll nip that in the bud, too.

First, let's set up our equipment. My choice would be a medium- to medium-heavy action rod and matching reel. Generally considered a small species for our inshore waters, most sea bass will range between a pound and three pounds, which would certainly allow us to employ a light-action rod and reel. However, you will often find yourself hauling up their heftier brothers and sisters from rocky inshore mussel beds, outcroppings, artificial reefs and ocean wrecks as well. Along our Atlantic coastline, black sea bass extend from Cape Cod to Cape Canaveral. You might find yourself fishing in five to fifty fathoms, so be prepared with a rig that can stand up to the rigors of rough bottom structure and strong currents. You could spool your reel with 15- to 20-pound test Ande monofilament (pink tends to be softer than clear) line, or you can use braided line in the same pound-test range but with its narrower diameter for greater line capacity and sensitivity. PowerPro braid is positively a winner. It's all a matter of preference. Donna likes monofilament; I like braid for this type of fishing. Several knots to know when handling braid come with PowerPro's packaging.

For terminal tackle on larger size black sea bass, I prefer Owner wide gap hooks ranging from 1/0 to 3/0—the type of hook commonly used for fluke. Many tackle shops sell pre-packaged snelled sea bass hooks that are labeled Porgy/Sea Bass hooks, size #6 or #7, and that is fine for porgies because they have small mouths. Too, that size hook would prove fine for those pound- to three-pound sea bass that a good many inshore anglers are accustomed to catching. But there are beauties to be had in deeper bodies of water, like Ron Atkinson's 24½ inch black sea bass taken just shy of three miles out of Shinnecock Inlet in fourteen fathoms. Mr. Atkinson was targeting fluke with a combination of long strips of squid and Portuguese spearing, which are larger than our typical spearing—*menidia*; i.e., Atlantic Silversides. A common porgy hook might not have landed this hefty five-pounder. Hence, a 1/0 to 3/0 wide gap type hook is the ticket; be it for fluke or blackfish, it will do double-duty on respectable sized black sea bass.

An excellent catalog to have on hand is one from Terminal Tackle Company, Inc. The shop is located at 120 Main Street in Kings Park, N. Y. 11754. The phone number is 631-269-6005; Web site: www.terminaltackleco.com. The first section of the catalog covers fishhooks. As there is no true industry standard referencing the specific size of fishhooks, the booklet clearly depicts actual sizes and shapes of a number of hooks offered from several leading manufacturers. Manufacturers of fishhooks are many. Stick with names such as Mustad, Gamakatsu, Owner, Eagle Claw and VMC.

Depending on the current, you should have 2- to 20-ounce bank sinkers on hand at all times. In depths of fifty fathoms, it is not uncommon to employ 16 ounces of lead, which I find utterly unwieldy. However, there is a sensible way around this weighty problem, which we'll tackle in the next chapter, but first things first.

Of course, plying the brine in 80 or so feet with traditional equipment, fresh-cut baits and up to 10 ounces of lead poses little problem. A conventional outfit along with a single hook, line and sinker will serve fittingly. Sea bass will greedily gobble up clam, squid and spearing. Fresh or fresh-frozen bait is important. Blood worms and sand worms are also excellent baits but a bit pricy. The rule of thumb is to use smaller hooks and lighter sinkers if we are talking a pound to three-pound lightweights as found in our area bays. Utilize heavier outfits and terminal tackle if you have heavyweights on your mind and menu as you go deeper into the ocean.

Rig terminal tackle for black sea bass as you would for blackfish (covered in the preceding chapter) by tying the main line (braid) to one end of a barrel swivel (rated for 50-pound test line) and employing a uni-knot. With a 3-foot length of 20- to 25-pound test monofilament or fluorocarbon, tie the leader material to the other end of a barrel swivel by employing an improved clinch knot. At the bottom of the leader, make a wide enough loop to accommodate a wide range of bank sinkers; tie off the loop by employing a double surgeon's knot. Make a 3- to 4-inch dropper loop a foot above the sinker to accommodate the hook.

Other artificial lures such as bucktails and tins work well, too. Experiment with different colored lures such as silver, gold and chartreuse. Add a strip of squid and bounce the lure a foot or two off the bottom. A twitch of the rod tip will invite strikes. The moment that you feel a strike, lift the rod smartly to set the hook and reel steadily.

When presenting either bait or artificial lures, it is important to use a heavy enough sinker or jig that will keep your line perpendicular to the bottom—regardless of whether you are anchored or set up for a drift. It is not unusual to employ a 2- to 4-ounce sinker at the top or bottom of the tide then three hours later have to switch to 10 ounces or more as the current increases. Having an assortment of lead on hand will keep you in the proper holding pattern.

Some of the finest in sea fare awaits your table.

Before venturing into this realm, be sure to hook up with a well-maintained and equipped vessel, coupled with a knowledgeable captain and crew. If you are captaining your own vessel, always check sea conditions and draw up a float plan, letting a responsible person know your destination along with the time and place of return. Charts, GPS, and marine radio communication are a must. Safety should be your primary concern.

Chapter 18

SHIMANO'S SYSTEMS AT WORK & PLAY

Butterfly ~ Lucanus ~ Waxwing ~ Orca

Shimano—manufacturers of world-famous, fine quality fishing equipment—has designed four lightweight systems that unquestionably replace heavy-duty rods along with sizable reels, heavy lines, weighty sinkers and big baits that would seemingly tackle *Jaws*. As a result, the game has changed dramatically. Shimano's state-of the-art Systems has reeled us into the Twenty-First Century. For those of you who are absolutely anal and positively committed to the finest in high-quality, state-of-the-art equipment, that is, rods, reels, lines and lures, you need to examine Shmano's four lure Systems for jigging, sub-surface, and top-water action.

It is at this juncture and arena that we depart from combining Shimano reels with Shakespeare's Ugly Stik rods as discussed in earlier chapters. I did this, as I'm sure you recall, in order to save you monies so that you might put that savings toward Shimano's top-of-the-line spinning and bait-casting (conventional) reels. In entering Shimano's four-system series, I'd strongly suggest investing in matching their rods, reels, lines and lures for one main reason. The systems are <u>specifically designed</u> to work in concert with one another. This is especially pertains to their two true jigging systems: the Butterfly Jigging System and the Lucanus Jigging System. If you purchased any of the reels covered in those earlier chapters, you're pretty much set. It's now a matter of selecting corresponding rods.

While jigging, it's nice to have a rod butt that extends well into the hollow of your arm for comfortable, virtually tireless, up-and-down pumping action. When a rod's butt is too short, the angler is forced to extend it forward of his or her body, bringing about fatigue in a very *short* period of time. A longer butt section is but one of many well-thought-out features incorporated into Shimano's jigging rod designs. Their engineers have considered every inch of taper from butt cap to tip top in order to offer you unparalleled performance in a staggering selection of choices. The <u>action</u> (flex) achieved to cast and retrieve a lure, coupled to the <u>power</u> to move and fight a fish, are specifically balanced among all components; that is, rod, reel, line and lure.

As Shimano presents a myriad of rods from which to choose, you will, in essence, be purchasing a custom rod for any application imaginable. Although this may seem, on the surface, overwhelming, Shimano takes the guesswork out of selection.

For example, addressing Shimano's four basic systems, Butterfly, Lucanus, Waxwing and Orca, every lure falls within a range of sizes and weights with which to expressly match rod(s), reel(s) and line(s). You wind up with a truly balanced outfit. The <u>rods</u> we'll be matching to reels, lines and lures for spinning and casting both in salt water and fresh water for all four Shimano lure systems will fall into three groups: Shimano's Trevala, Tescata and Terez rods.

Let's first examine two fantastic state-of-the-art Shimano Jigging Systems that will positively help you circumvent that weighty problem of fishing with pound-plus sinkers in profound depths that are measured in fathoms in lieu of feet—and without bait! As a matter of pure unadulterated fact, there isn't a pelagic that swims that Shimano lures haven't taken. Yes, I'm talking fish from the oceans around the world. For example, cod, haddock, ling, tilefish, bluefin, yellowfin, red snapper, jack crevalle, dolphin, wahoo, billfish, red trout, et cetera. In our ocean and bays, Donna and I have nailed every species chapterized in this handbook. Let's begin with Shimano's Butterfly Jigging System.

Butterfly:

Within Shimano's Butterfly Jig Series, there are presently three styles: the Butterfly-**Whirligig**, the Butterfly-**Centervortex**, and the Butterfly-**Slidend**; six lengths/weights 2 oz., 2 5/8 oz., 3 1/8 oz. ($13.99); 3 7/8 oz., 4 ¾ oz., 5 5/8 oz. ($16.99); available in seven colors for all sizes.

For what exactly are these styles specifically designed?

The Butterfly-<u>Whirligig</u> moves through the water column with a spiraling action generated by a symmetric flat body design.

The Butterfly-<u>Centervortex</u> moves through the water column with very erratic (every which way but loose) motions generated by its rhombic body design. For example, a horizontal sideways falling action, a darting action, and a short sliding action.

The Butterfly-<u>Slidend</u> moves through the water column with a side-to-side action generated by a hexahedral body design.

Shimano's Trevala jigging rod series, available in both casting and spinning, are specifically designed for Butterfly jigs. I married Shimano's TFS-63M spinning 6'3" Trevala Butterfly rod to a **H**igh **E**fficiency **G**earing (**HEG**) Stella SW spinning reel, model 5000. Pictured on the following page is the rod and reel with a 3 7/8 oz. Whirligig in Brown/Silver.

Shimano Trevala Butterfly rod, Stella SW 5000 reel
Butterfly Whirligig, Brown/Silver, 4 ¾ inches, 3 7/8 ounces

Although discontinued, earlier versions of Shimano's Butterfly jigging lures may still be found by searching the internet for three basic styles: <u>Regular</u> Jigs, <u>Long</u> Jigs, and <u>Flat-Side</u> asymmetric jigs.

The <u>Regular</u> 3-D jigs were available in eight lengths/weights (2 oz., 2 5/8 oz., 3 1/8 oz., 3 7/8 oz., 4 ¾ oz., 5 5/8 oz., 7 oz., 9 ½ oz.); six colors for each size.

The <u>Long</u> 3-D jigs were available in two lengths/weights (4¼ oz., 7 oz.); eight colors for each size.

The <u>Flat-Side</u> 3-D jigs were available in six lengths/weights (4 oz., 5oz., 6 oz., 8 oz., 10 oz., 12 oz.); twelve colors for each size.

For what exactly were the three groups specifically designed?

The <u>Regular</u> series has a spiral, darting action on retrieve. The <u>Long</u> series has a roll-wobble motion on descent coupled to an exaggerated side-to-side long-distance horizontal darting display on retrieve so as to catch the attention of predators suspended anywhere in the water column. The <u>Flat-Side</u> series has a swinging motion on descent and is specifically designed for angle-vertical jigging while drifting from a boat. The lure displays a commonplace eye on the one side and an off-set eye positioned approximately three-quarters rearward on the other side.

Google the internet for these three style jigs, too. If and when you locate them in a size and color that may fit your need, grab them.

Lucanus:

Lucanus Jigging Lures (left to right) 7 oz., 5¼ oz., 3½ oz., 3 oz., 2oz.

Shimano's Lucanus jig method of fishing is a system tailor-made for deep-water fishing. Just imagine a 3½-ounce jig tackling what it would take 12 ounces of lead to do in 120 feet; or a 7-ounce jig descending to the depth of 300 feet where it would take a pound of lead or better to hold your line perpendicular to the bottom. An angler could go even deeper by drop-shot rigging; that is, attaching at least a 7-foot monofilament leader to a second eyelet located on the bottom of a Lucanus aero-hydrodynamic head-design jig, attaching either another jig or a sinker. Two 1/0 Owner hooks are obscured within the silicon skirt and trailers of each lure. Lucanus glow-eyed jigs are available in five weights: 2, 3, 3½ ($14.99); 5¼ and 7 ounces ($17.99). Too, these lures come in eight color combinations within each weight category: blue/silver, chartreuse/white, green/gold, black/gold, orange/white, purple/red, pink/white, and brown/chartreuse.

The complete baitcasting setup for the Lucanus system incorporates Shimano's Calcutta TE 400 LJV reel (conventional round) and matching Tescata rods —medium light, medium, and medium heavy—expressly designed with specific tapers to accommodate the range of Lucanus jig weights. Shimano also offers a Lucanus spinning rod and reel system.

It is practically a guarantee that if you board a boat with a party of offshore anglers unfamiliar with the Lucanus system, you are sure to be ridiculed for bringing what would first *appear* to be a poor excuse of a rod that couldn't possibly tax a feisty catfish in fresh water. The wimpy-looking noodle-like wand is coupled to a deceivingly lightweight jig version reel that would seem more at home on our bays than on the ocean—not to mention a selection of weird-looking lures that would ostensibly stand a better chance of holding bottom in a flushed toilet!

"What do you mean, you don't need bait?" one skeptic in the group will surely ask. "No squid? No spearing? What do you expect to catch with that beetle-like bug? Ya kiddin' us or what?"

Yet, lo and behold, you are sure to outfish your buddies—and with considerably less effort. To me, reeling up 16-plus ounces of lead from fifty fathoms sounds a lot less like fishing and more like work. Tescata jigging rods' TC$_4$ construction is wrapped in cutting-edge technology. Double inner layers of advanced dynamic T Glass, along with an inner and outer spiral of high modulus graphite comprise these rod blanks. They are powerful tools, yet sensitive enough to feel every tick, bump, tap and take. Too, the Calcutta TE 400 LJV (**Lucanus Jig Version**) reel can apply the brakes at a maximum drag of 16 pounds. That is some serious stopping power built into a 13.3-ounce housing and handle. You will want to spool with 20- to 50- pound test braid for added line capacity as well as unparalleled sensitivity. Again, your choice should be PowerPro braided line. Visit www.lucanusjig.com for more information.

But what is a Lucanus lure exactly? It is the main component of this unique jigging system, taking on a profile that resembles a cross between a big bug and a squid. The lure is named after the Lucanus, a well-known species of stag or New World scarab beetle. The jig's body shape suggests the mantle of a squid or baby octopus. It is a strange looking bugger but works like a charm.

Two 1/0 Owner Dancing Stinger hooks are concealed within the silicon skirt and trailers of the larger lures, two 3/0 Owner Dancing Stinger hooks for the smaller jigs. Lucanus glow-eyed jigs have elongated appendages for better visibility in deep water. Preferences of jig colors will vary geographically and from season to season. For example, bottom fish feed on crabs in the middle of winter, and then start feeding on baitfish in early spring. Experimenting with different patterns and weights for different species is always fun and exciting. I may pick pink/white or purple/red come late fall and into winter, then switch to blue/silver or green/gold come springtime. I nailed a half-dozen cocktail blues in half an hour on a 2 oz. orange/white pattern in our bay toward the end of summer. Donna pulled up three double-digit doormats and many shorts from the ocean floor in a matter of a couple of hours using a 3½ oz. chartreuse/white pattern.

The jigging procedure consists of a five-step technique: 1) Freespool the jig to the bottom. 2) Start winding very slowly. 3) Work the jig through the appropriate water column. 4) Drop the jig anew. 5) Repeat the process. The initial taps is the fish biting on the lure's skirt and trailers. Allow the fish to work its way up to the stinger hooks. Keep reeling until the fish hooks itself. Then lift the rod smartly to set the hook(s) firmly, reeling steadily. *Voilà*! If you haven't owned or handled Owner stinger hooks, there is only one way to do so—most carefully. They are extremely sharp. Upon examination of Lucanus' Multiple Hook System, you will quickly understand why there is no need for larger hooks; the pair will do the job quite nicely. Trust me on this. The #3 is perfect for the three smaller jigs. The #1/0 is ideal for the two larger jigs.

Shimano Lucanus Green/Gold, 7-ounce Jig

Pictured above is Shimano's Tescata TSC63**MH** 6'3" **M**edium-**H**eavy Fast Action rod conjoined to Shimano's Calcutta TE 400 LJV **L**ucanus **J**ig **V**ersion levelwind workhorse, loaded with a 7-ounce purple/red Lucanus jig.

Waxwing (saltwater series):

Although classified as a jig, Shimano's Waxwings are *not* traditionally designed to be dropped overboard then worked vertically in the water column. Instead, they are sub-surface casting saltwater swimming/darting missiles that take wing before erratically making their way back to the angler. The Saltwater Series come in five sizes:

The **Baby** Waxwing is 2.7" long and weighs ½ oz. ($14.99). The Waxwing **Boy** is 3.5" and weighs 7/8 oz. ($17.99). The Waxwing **Junior** is 4.6" and weighs 1½ oz. ($19.99). The Waxwing **Senior** is 5.4" and weighs 3.1 oz. (also $19.99). The Waxwing **Daddy** is 6.6" and weighs 4.4 oz. ($22.99). With the exception of big Daddy, all Waxwings come in fourteen colors. Daddy is available in eight colors. It is best to consult their online catalog for colors and shades thereof.

The Waxwing gets its name from the translucent wax-like fins located above and below the head of the lure. Its swimming action is controlled by the speed of the retrieve. I employ a faster retrieve in order to send the imitation's side-to-side zigzag motion followed by an irregular kicking movement. The Waxwing is best worked by casting then pointing the rod tip directly at the lure, not off to the side. The Waxwing's frenetic swimming, darting and kicking action will send predator fish into a feeding frenzy if not simply an instinctive reaction strike.

The bottom wing keeps the lure upright while the top wing creates its erratic, wobbly motion. It's the design of the jig's head coupled to the top wing that hydrodynamically produces the darting effect as the imitation travels through the water column. Fixating on the Waxwings side-to-side motion, this single-bodied beauty has the incredible action of what only my jointed-bodied lures can even come close to producing. But to wobble forward then additionally dance off as if affecting its escape, well, that's a lure that certainly belongs in your bag of tricks.

Through-construction wiring along with Owner double-pronged saltwater hooks, 3-X strong and—believe me—super, super sharp, ensures quality. The Baby, Boy, Junior and Senior are tailed with two-pronged hooks. The Daddy tails a single free-swinging hook.

Shimano's Terez rods are specifically designed to cast Waxwings. Coupled with conventional high-speed reels such as the Curado 300 E7 (7 bearings) series low-profile conventional reels, or Stella, Sustain and Stradic spinning reel models, you're in the right arena. Shimano suggests the larger Curado 300 EJ for launching the heavier Senior and Daddy Waxwings. Pictured below is the Terez TZCW-X80MH-**A** (**A**qua) 8 foot Medium-Heavy, Extra Fast Action rod, expressly aimed at launching the 1½ ounce Waxwing Junior. The rod is wedded to a Curado model 301E series (left hand) reel (also available as a right-hand model).

Shimano Waxwing Jr., Bunker, 4.6 inches, 1½ ounces

Waxwings (freshwater series):

Shimano has recently expanded its market and put out a line of freshwater Waxwing lures, available in two sizes and weights corresponding to the saltwater versions of the Senior and Daddy. However, the freshwater series come in eight different colors than the fourteen colors offered in the saltwater series. It is best to consult Shimano's online catalog for colors and shades thereof.

These two, new freshwater Waxwing lures are aimed particularly at musky and pike.

Orca: (saltwater series)

Newest in Shimano's lineup of lures are the Orca top-water pencil baits, which come in two sizes and are available in six colors: Blue Sardine, Clear Silver, Green Mack, Black Silver, Purple Gold, Pink Silver. The 2-ounce lure measures 6.3 inches ($24.99); the 3-ounce lure measures 7.5 inches ($29.99). Although engineered as a surface lure, a moderate retrieve while jerking the rod tip will make the lure pop and dive, simulating a wounded baitfish. While at rest the Orca hangs in the brine at a 45-degree angle with only its nose and eyes showing above the surface, affecting its demise. I cast out and allow the lure to sit for a moment upon the suds then jerk the rod tip three or four times to have that *wounded baitfish* pop and dive, retrieving and repeating the action all the way back to shore or boat. Orca's action in the water column is generated by a hydrodynamically designed internal weight while functioning aerodynamically when casting long distances. As with all Shimano lures (Butterfly, Lucanus, Waxwing), only the best hardware is employed to make the Orca bulletproof. Ultra-sharp, high-tensile strength treble hooks coupled to heavy-duty split rings ensure longevity. Cheap? Not by a long shot. Quality? That's what you're paying for.

As part of the System, Orca lures are best launched by either of two 7'8" Terez spinning rods; that is, Shimano's **H**eavy, Medium Fast-Action TZS78**H** or their E**x**tra-**H**eavy, Medium Fast-Action TZS78**XH**. These rods are well suited to the Stella and Sustain high-speed spinning reels series. Pictured below are Shimano's Stella SW 5000, a larger Stella SW 8000 model, along with a 2-ounce Orca, Blue Sardine colored lure and a 3-ounce Black Back Silver killer. These superior systems can handle virtually anything swimming in our inshore waters. Launching and delivering Orcas to blitzing pelagic game fish, Shimano's even larger Stella SW series spinning reels coupled to the E**x**tra-**H**eavy, Medium Fast-Action TZS78**XH** can tackle the job. This System is for the serious angler hunting some serious size fish.

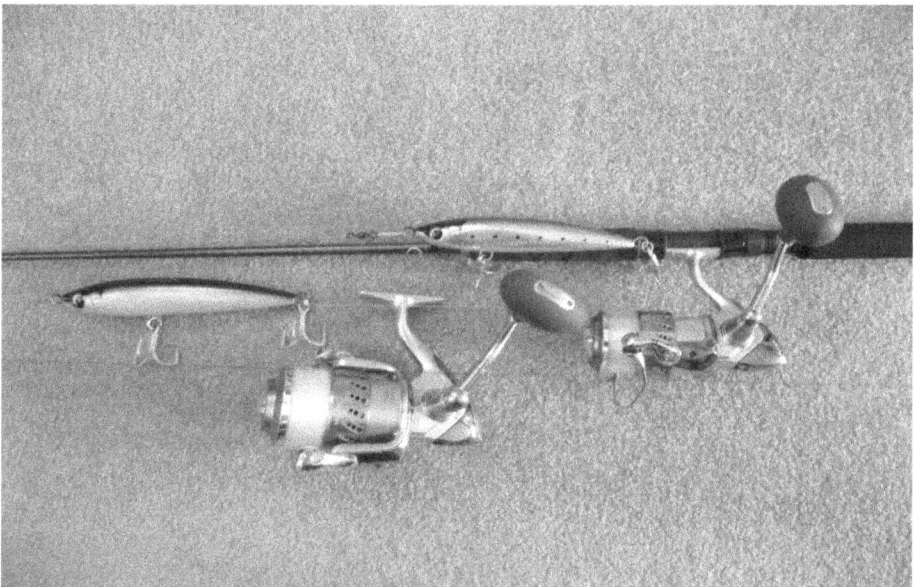

Note that a conventional rod/reel setup is not recommended by Shimano. Both the Stella and Sustain spinning reel models are the preferred outfits.

After casting and "walking the dog," snap the rod tip downward, causing the lure to pop and dive momentarily, creating a side-by-side rolling motion before resurfacing. Quickly retrieve the pencil popper, pause, then repeat the process. You are going to drive predator fish wild. As a picture is worth a thousand words, consult Shimano's online catalog for exacting colors and shades thereof to match the hatch.

Chapter 19

KAYAKS & CANOES

Fishing from a kayak allows one to move through skinny waters where many a craft would simply dread to thread their way along a scabrous shoreline. One of the obvious reasons is for fear that captain and crew could run the risk of being left high and not necessarily dry because rocks are, indeed, hard! Also, a more prudent captain operating a boat with even a shallow two-foot draft while plying deeper waters could, without warning, suddenly find himself stranded upon a sand bar for a spell. But such a shore that is lined with rocks and boulders, including those inviting shallow cutouts that hold and trap baitfish—not to mention a pass through the very trough paralleling that particularly promising shoal—provide perfect ambush points for big bass. These inshore areas are precisely where sizable stripers abound come dusk and early dawn.

Of course, each fishing platform has its advantages and disadvantages, no different than each type of rod and reel has a specific application—be it a spinning outfit, a baitcasting setup, or a fly rod and reel. As a kayak is the personification of stealth, a light- to medium-action spinning outfit, and especially a fly rod, complete the picture and fit the bill like a hand in glove. If you want to limit the competition, find peace and solitude (that is until the action hits nonstop) you simply cannot beat fishing from a kayak. "Well," you might ask, "what about fishing from a canoe?" True enough, I'll answer. However, I much prefer fishing from a kayak, especially a sit-on-top type (SOT), over that of a canoe, and for an important reason. Safety. You are centered upon a more stable platform when fishing from a SOT yak than when seated in a tippy canoe. Unless you don't mind dropping to your knees and remaining in that position until the fight with a very big fish is finished, I'd rule out a canoe.

I have caught bucket-mouthed sized bass from both kayak and canoe; it's really no big deal. But I've also been on those Nantucket sleigh rides, being pulled around and along both bay and coastal waters by several bruiser blues while fighting them in both sit-on-top (SOTs) and sit-in-side (SINKs) kayaks as well as a few canoes. In such a situation, I am considerably safer in a kayak than a canoe when engaging one of those choppers. On more than one occasion, while fishing from a canoe, I thought that I was going to have to finish the fight eyeball-to-eyeball, literally, *in* as well as *on* their turf. Generally speaking, I feel that canoes are more for touring, whereas kayaks are the preferred platform for fishing. During the heat of battle in a kayak designed for fishing, although practically eye to eye with your challenger, you are rewarded a whole new perspective. Unlike sitting or standing within the cockpit of a traditional powerboat, or even a rowboat, you'll certainly find the kayak experience quite unique.

Like anything new, kayak paddling takes a little getting used to. It's a bit different than moving through the water with a canoe. With some instruction, which most kayak dealers are more than happy to provide, along with the requisite and inevitable practice on your part, you will become proficient. This is not brain surgery. So, let's decide how to intelligently go about selecting your fishing kayak and, most importantly, too, the basic two-bladed paddle. Keep in mind that *not* so age-old adage: different strokes for different folks. In short, no pun intended, consider a short paddle with pronounced curved blades in order for you to execute powerful strokes through some serious rough whitewater fishing, such as targeting ocean reefs. Conversely, select a more conventional, longer shaft, narrower-bladed paddle with a flatter surface for inshore action.

As there is no such thing as the *perfect* fishing machine coupled to its power plant, it holds true that there is no such thing as the perfect kayak, canoe, et cetera. But let's try to come as close as we can in picking out our ideal people-powered fishing machine. We're already halfway there, truly, because we know what we want to do with this vessel, and that is, fish, fish, fish! Remember, first and foremost, we're after a *stable* fishing platform.

Next, let's determine where you are going to use this nimble little gem. Are you going to fish the brine; that is, the back bays, along its shores, through coastal inlets, estuaries, rivers and such? Or are you a freshwater fishing fool who will be content to paddle small lakes, big ponds, perhaps brackish waters leading up to one of those saltier bodies? If you limit your horizon to one watery arena or the other, size, particularly length, will most definitely figure into your equation. But why shortchange yourself? Why not consider the best of both worlds? Why not imagine yourself fishing a large pond one day and then a good size bay the next. I believe the best all-around length for a fishing kayak is 12 to 13 feet; that's my preference. I can easily sweep (turn) the craft in a relatively narrow space on a calm or brisk day. Additionally, I've witnessed guys and gals in these same vessels whipping through the white waters of the Atlantic, a good distance from shore, sprinting out of harm's way while fishing an ocean reef. This, however, would not be within my comfort zone. I've pounded through 2½ footers out at and around Robins Island, and that's about as high as I wish to be tossed in a kayak or a canoe. I'm not interested in pushing the envelope. I would just like you to be aware that there is such a realm of aficionados *out there*. This is extreme whitewater fishing for the stout of heart. Note that I did not say the unsound of mind; not at all. For these men and women are extremely knowledgeable with regard to handling their kayaks in untoward conditions. This will give you some idea of just how stable and seaworthy these crafts really are. To further the point, let's take a peek back into time.

In essence, a kayak *is* a kind of canoe of Inuit derivation, traditionally constructed from the skins of seals and other such sea mammals that were then stretched along a wooden and/or whalebone framework. Ancestors of the Inuit date back some five thousand years, whereby the Paleo-Eskimos from the Bering Straits came to the Arctic Coast of Alaska, descending into the Northwest Territories. Thousands of years later, in Ireland, Wales, and the western parts of England, currachs and coracles—that is, old but venerable craft dating back to the early fifteenth and mid-sixteenth centuries—were initially comprised of wickerwork covered with animal skins. Subsequently, they were interwoven with laths of more modern materials such as canvas and other tarred or oiled cloths. When we think of canoes during days of old, we probably conjure up images of the American Indian kneeling and paddling in dugout logs, or more lightweight structures framed in birch bark. But the Inuit peoples, ranging from northern Alaska to eastern Canada and Greenland (succeeding their ancestors, the Dorsets and then the Thules), are credited with the innovation and refinement of the kayak. As a matter of fact, kayak, meaning "hunter's boat," is what the vessel was primarily used for, as the 'catch of the day' was caribou, seal, walrus, and even whale! Now, that's what I call a hunting/fishing expedition!

Whereas the Inuit people constructed these amazing seaworthy vessels to work such treacherous, frigid northern waters—perilous in the sense that capsizing the craft could buy you no more than three minutes before hypothermia took its toll and shut your body down—you, dear reader, have the benefit of twenty-first century technology. Your kayak is not held together by entrails and patchwork. Most kayaks of today are made of a solid plastic (polyethylene) that can take a bit of beating off a boulder should you wish to play around ocean reefs or the like. You can adjust a pair of trigger-lock foot braces to offer comfort and good support. You can choose the vessel's overall length and width to ensure a stable fishing platform as you pursue your quarry for food and/or sport, be it *Morone saxatilis* or *Pomatomus saltatrix*: striped bass and bluefish, respectively. Too, you even have a choice of colors for your craft. I good-humoredly berated one company in particular for not offering *seal* blue after they kept pushing teal blue. I don't think they caught the significance or my attempt at strained humor.

What is not a joke is that there are still people in the far northern region of Greenland who hunt whale in their traditional kayaks, and when they have the unfortunate experience of capsizing and dying as a result of that event, the Inuit folk say that it is simply because "the person used someone else's kayak," a kayak that wasn't made specifically for that particular individual, a kayak that "didn't have the same sense of balance." The point I'm leading up to is that if you are two hundred fifty pounds, and I'm one hundred sixty pounds, I'd bet good money that we're going to select different kayaks from our local dealer after testing several types and models. We'd be foolish if we bought blindly, even if an acquaintance or our best friend said, "I love my kayak; this one is most definitely the one for you."

Now, here is a misconception many folks have regarding sit-on-top kayaks. They see scuppers along the plastic platform: stern, cockpit and bow. Consequently, they envision themselves sitting in a shallow pool of water. This is not the case. The water does not rise above the scuppers unless you were to exert enough pressure to cause it to happen. For example, with a thickness of five inches between top and bottom in the stern area of my yak, you can—when bearing down upon the platform at dockside, and with considerable force—exert enough pressure to force water up the scuppers and into that aft area, which would immediately drain on release. Mid-ship, with a depth of eight-inch scuppers adjacent to each side of the seat, I defy you to force water up into that area; you can't. Whatever water does enter the yak, whether from heavy rainfall or over-the-bow and/or under-the-keel wave action, immediately drains through those scuppers. You are actually drier than if you were sitting in a sit-in type kayak, which collects water and does not drain. Therefore, you would need a portable hand pump to empty water from a sit-in type yak.

Common sense dictates that your season is going to be somewhat limited whether you select a sit-on-top or a sit-in type kayak, merely because you are going to get a bit wet at some point—not necessarily drenched. For instance: the action of paddling allows a slight column of water to trail and trickle from blade to shaft and land in your lap. Those rubber paddle drip rings on the shaft help out somewhat but not completely. This intrusion may be somewhat welcome during a hot July or August day, but not in November or December, and certainly not in January or February. You do not want to be braving the elements during those cold and bitter months, although you certainly could with the right outfit—namely, a wet suit or dry suit. It's not really my thing . . . yet. Although the trunk of your body is exposed in a sit-on-top yak, kayak clothing, whether selecting a wet suit or half wet suit (top or bottoms), lightweight or insulated, depending on air and water temperature, is your ticket to to keeping warm and/or dry. For cold weather, not frigid, I simply layer clothing for desired comfort then don a Gore-Tex outfit (jacket and/or pants), which is both breathable and waterproof. Good to go.

During the middle of January of 2007, Donna and I paddled the Peconic River in our 16½-foot Mad River canoe from the navigable headwater beginning in Manorville, heading east to the town of Riverhead. It was January 16th, the day before the temperature suddenly plummeted into the teens. As a matter of fact, the mercury was rapidly falling by late afternoon when we arrived in town. Up until that point, all of us here on Long Island had been enjoying a mild winter. A mild mid-January or not, we would not have wanted to make that meandering twelve-mile journey dressed in street clothes while paddling a sit-on-top kayak. Therefore, our touring canoe was the ticket because we were a bit more protected. Likewise, that same trip along the Peconic in a sit-in kayak would have been a breeze had there been a light wind or a blow of twenty knots primarily because your torso and legs are protected from the elements.

But back to the issue of safety, for it is and should be of paramount importance to all of us while plying any body of water. Which is the *safer* vessel between a sit-in and a sit-on-top yak? If you are kayaking in an area with big boat traffic, I can almost guarantee that some captain, either careless or inconsiderate, is going to leave you in his or her wake—a situation that may or may not result in your taking on water or, worse yet, swamping and capsizing you. Therefore, unless you know exactly what you're doing, you could find yourself in over your head—literally.

As a sit-on-top kayak is self-bailing, it is a relatively simple procedure for a fit person to climb back aboard if capsized. Not so with a sit-in. The cockpit is going to fill, and unless you know a few safety procedures, you could find yourself in dire straits. Perhaps not as bad a situation as if you were in the Bering Straits or in those other northerly areas mentioned above, but bad enough. The Inuit people had air-filled seal bladders to lend buoyancy to their craft. Aftermarket foam-filled bags can be purchased for your sit-in craft should you decide to go that route. Check this out with your local kayak/canoe dealer. Concerning sit-in-type yaks, you should seek out instruction in learning a maneuver or two that could save life or limb. So that you'll have a reference, the Eskimo roll is one. An instructor will more than likely teach you others. Also, for beginners it would be wise to travel in pairs or a group and learn rescue techniques. It would be prudent to practice these techniques with one another: rescuer and victim. Confidence is definitely cool.

In all fairness referencing sit-on-top type kayaks, I have a fair-weather friend (meteorologically speaking) who simply loves her Wilderness Systems Pamlico 145T (tandem) almost as much as she loves her cat. And that's saying something. Another friend enjoys his sit-in Wilderness Systems Pungo 120; 12 feet long, 29 inches wide, 52-pounds. However, those shells are more for playing around the water on temperate days and in calm waters. They are not serious fishing platforms.

Homing in on the Right Kayak—for <u>You</u>

Donna on our Yak

You now have a fairly good idea between a sit-in and sit-on-top yak. I had mentioned earlier that we are halfway there in selecting the right kayak for you because we know, predominately, what we want to do with that platform, and that is to fish. A sit-on-top yak is better suited to this endeavor, and not only from a safety factor. You'll have a clearer understanding as we move along.

It seems that there are more manufacturers and models of kayaks on the market today than "Carter has little liver pills." Choosing the right angling yak can be an overwhelming experience. Fortunately, we can narrow the field even further by focusing in on reputable manufacturers whose selection features or offers optional equipment and accoutrements set up with the angler in mind: flush-mounted rod holders astern, additional fully adjustable-lockable-removable rod holder brackets set forward, a comfortable seat and backrest, ample storage space, an anchor trolley system, and a combo unit GPS/Fishfinder. Why all this paraphernalia? The answer is because we ideally want the *ultimate* fishing platform and equipment.

A rudder option may also be available, something that you might want to consider when outfitting your kayak for fishing. What I absolutely *need* to outfit a kayak versus what I would *like* could be worlds apart. Remember, you only have so much space aboard; and for the most part, you take up a good portion of it.

By selecting a kayak set up with the angler in mind, we have just ruled out the explorer class, the tandem touring type, and the wild-and-wooly whitewater adventure craft. How come? Because the explorer class calls for a longer, narrower vessel to propel one along greater distances; stability is not its virtue. The tandem touring model is not designed for, nor conducive to fishing; as such, it would prove a deliberate attempt for two people to get in each other's way. Lastly, the considerably shorter whitewater craft is configured so as to subsume turn-on-a-dime maneuverability for psyched-up folks who live to ply swift currents and shoot rapids. Let's now home in on the breed of yak that lends itself to the true art of angling—be it spin, bait, or fly-fishing—while at the same time addresses the issue of safety.

I feel that sit-in type yaks (SINKs) are fair-weather cruising vessels. For serious fishing, sit-on-top yaks (SOTs), which are self-bailing, are true fishing platforms that are meant to be paddled in a variety of sea conditions—from fair to foul. In my opinion, the advantages of a sit-on-top kayak outweigh those of the sit-in model. If you are in agreement at this point, we've narrowed the decision-making process considerably.

Selecting the Right SOT—for <u>You</u>

Next, let's weigh speed versus stability versus weight. I know a savvy fishing fellow who raves about his Ocean Kayak Prowler Angler Edition 15-foot 4.5-inch long, 28.5-inch wide, 56-pound shell. I have a pal who swears by his 13-foot Hobie Quest; another fellow who predominately pedals (versus paddles) the same company's Wave Walker model. The first fellow mentioned with the 15-foot Ocean Kayak selected his yak by simply weighing speed against stability. The vessel is propelled from point A to point B lickety-split. And that's exactly what the man wants his craft to do—move quickly. I prefer a bit shorter length and broader beam for stability.

Again, it is important to keep three basics in mind when narrowing your selection. Longer, narrower yaks are faster and cover greater distances with less effort. Shorter yaks are lighter and more maneuverable in tight quarters. Wider yaks offer stable platforms. Understanding these three variables and applying them according to the kind of fishing you are going to do will help to determine which yak is right for you.

Let's examine an interesting hybrid. There's a relatively new kayak on the market that is a combination sit-on-top kayak/canoe (but without scuppers) which is, in essence, still a sit-in yak of sorts. Its freeboard appears impressive and the platform looks—as the manufacturer boasts—"very open, yet completely dry." Initially, I liked this concept a lot. However, let's take a closer look at this innovative kayak-like hull conjoined to a canoe-like cockpit from Mad River Canoe. Doug Murphy, proprietor of Eagle's Neck Paddling Company in Southold, had brought one to our club, Eastern Flyrodders of Long Island, in Riverhead. The Synergy 12 model is 12-feet long with a beam of 30.8 inches, weighing in at 60 pounds. It's an interesting fishing platform, but we must not stop here. Remember, we're only shopping at this point. MSRP was $750. I say "was" because Mad River no longer manufactures this hybrid model.

Before you run out and purchase this or any platform and be accused of impulse buying, you want to know how *you* fit into the form. Are you truly comfortable? How does the vessel track through the water? What type of double-bladed paddle would work to its best advantage? These are all very important considerations. Ah, as seal blue is not an option, will you be happy with mango or a natural sand color? In other words, do you wish to stand out and be seen in crowded waters, or do you wish to blend within a serene setting? Addressing kayak safety first and foremost, you do *not* want to blend in with your surroundings; rather, you want to stand out and be seen. The fish won't mind. Hence, a bright color choice is a wise choice.

After considering several sit-on-top yaks for angling purposes, one kept resurfacing in my mind and notes. I opted for an Ocean Kayak Prowler <u>Big Game Angler</u>, measuring in at 12 feet 9 inches long, 34 inches wide, and a whopping 69 pounds. That's 13 pounds more than that fellow's 15-plus foot Ocean Kayak Prowler <u>Angler Edition</u> model. That's a lot of weight to haul around, but I knew where I was going to use the craft predominately, that is, on the Peconic River [where I reside] and its neighboring bays. Weight, therefore, was not such an important factor; width for better stability was. Admittedly, if I had to transport that vessel from place to place on a regular basis atop my vehicle and/or portage that behemoth any significant distance, it would be the end of the story—and maybe me! So, that beautiful Ocean Kayak Prowler Big Game Angler is not for everyone. But it is for *moi*. It is a serious person-powered fishing machine. MSRP is $980.

Two other companies that manufacture fine sit-on-top yaks designed for fishing are Wilderness Systems and Malibu Kayaks. Once you are satisfied with your selection from bow to stern, make certain the vessel has at least a pair of rod holders strategically placed in a position that will aid in the type of fishing you have in mind, be it spin, bait, or fly-fishing. I carry all three outfits when I'm out for a full day of kayak fishing. I wouldn't leave home without them. Many of these kayaks already have a set of molded-in rod holders to accommodate spin and baitcasting rods; however, you may wish to add a handy base-mounted removable snap-on/snap-off style rod holder in front of the cockpit. Some models accommodate a fly rod and reel. This will allow you access to that invaluable short-butted wand that just won't fit in a conventional deck-mounted holder. Keep in mind that you can always customize your craft later.

Additionally, I carry a folding grapnel anchor along with 50 feet of line, billy club, knife, pliers, nailclipper, gloves, cellular phone, compass, whistle, head lamp, rain gear, polarized sunglasses, along with an extra set of clothing in a dry storage bag. Most of these items are neatly packed into a milk crate that's lashed into the stern. Be sure to purchase a paddle leash for insurance. Too, it would be a good idea to buy additional leashes for your rods. Most importantly, I wear a PFD (personal flotation device) life vest. On hot sunny days, I don a cachalot; that is, a long-brimmed hat (with drawcord) designed to protect both face and neck.

On the North Fork of Long Island, there are two fantastic dealers who can help you make an informed decision. I have already mentioned Doug Murphy of Eagle's Neck Paddling Company in Southold. Jim Dreeben of the Peconic Paddler in Riverhead is the other fellow (but nearing retirement). Both men are extremely knowledgeable and great guys to deal with. They'll steer you in the right direction. On the South Fork, in East Quogue at Dockers Waterside Marina, is Captain Kayak. Back west, in Sayville, is Stein's Marina.

Kayaking has come a long way. Not to complicate matters, but to give you some idea, there are kayaks out there (one that I mentioned earlier) that you pedal rather than paddle. The propulsion system is chain driven, much like a bicycle. I've seen several in for repair. Too, there are motorized kayaks operated by battery. You can make things complicated, or you can stay in keeping with the theme of this book: KISS. Keep It Simple System. Once again—different strokes for different folks.

Well, that's enough yakking about kayaks and canoes, but I'll conclude by reiterating on last important point. And that is to try before you buy and ply your favorite waters, keeping in mind that here in the northeast we live in a fishing mecca.

Chapter 20

CLAMMING

Clams (quahogs) make for fine fare—from appetizers, to soups, to magnificent main courses. Clamming is really a simple process requiring little more than a decent clam rake, a container (be it made of plastic, wood, wire or whatever), a buoyant support in which to set and float the container, and a length of line running from the container to your waist to pull along your prizes as you rake bottom structure. Additionally, you'll want to check the local regulations for Shellfish Harvest Areas, as you may need a permit or license. For productive clamming, simply work a sandy-muddy shoreline, the periphery of a sandbar, or in-between patches of eel grass. The further away from traffic—be it bathers, other clam diggers, boats, et cetera—the better.

Unless you want to look at this activity as a form of labor instead of a labor of love, arrange your schedule to coincide with working one hour on each side of a low tide. This way you're sure to score without becoming enervated and/or sore. Two hours is a good amount of time to collect a decent amount of clams for the table, which should provide many a meal for family and guests. If the pickings proved slow from the get-go, or you're a bit greedy, you can always elect to continue for another hour or so. A moment or two of instruction is all that is needed to operate a clam rake efficiently. In a matter of a couple of outings, you'll probably be able to discern the difference between a rock and a clam as you scratch away at the watery floor for quahogs.

Quahogs are a general term relating to the family of edible clams having a relatively hard shell. Littlenecks, cherrystones, topnecks and chowders comprise the list. However, there is a bit of confusion leading to a heap of controversy as to size order. Some folks argue that topnecks are larger than littlenecks (true) but smaller than cherrystones (not necessarily true). By strict definition, topnecks are actually larger than cherrystones; region determines interpretation. Even its spelling is argued in some instances; sometimes shown as two words: top necks.

To belabor the issue and to have a little fun, I set forth the argument in one of my novels titled *The Author*. The setting is a Sicilian restaurant on the south shore of Long Island. A mafia boss and his henchman, both customers enjoying dinner, argue the point insistently. Who is right? The *boss* (our parents frequently told us) is always right. Right? Well, in this case, the boss' henchman's family were Bonackers (blue collar folks from the south shore of Long Island who had for generations made their living from fishing and clamming) and, therefore, knew better. The argument escalates and is presented to a tactful waitress who, right or wrong, realizes that the *customer* is always right. But which customer—the mafia don or his henchman? The waitress resourcefully addresses the dilemma when challenged by Don Ciccio as to what kind of clams were set before him. She simply states, "I believe *you* [Don Ciccio] call them topnecks."

That's pretty much the crux of the matter. It has become, for the most part, a regional issue or argument. In New England, it's unquestionable that a topneck is larger than a cherrystone. On Long Island, most folks insist that a topneck has found its niche between a littleneck and a cherrystone in size order. A good many fish markets in our area cull, grade, and sell them accordingly; that is, littlenecks being the most expensive per dozen, followed by topnecks, cherrystones, and then chowders. If you want to belabor and argue the point intelligently, go to the source for meanings and spellings. For openers, open an unabridged dictionary—as you probably won't find what you're looking for in a desk copy reference. Enough said. Now that I've shamelessly plugged one of my award-winning novels and made my point with regard to quahogs, permit me to relate a nonfictional account of how I came by my *hot* clamming spot. But first I must relate those frustrating early years.

Many a moon ago, Donna and I spent a couple of hours clamming in a supposed hot spot on the North Fork. We clammed with our feet and hands. After two man-hours of hard work, we managed to collect a dozen or so clams, mostly chowders. That evening, because of our indefatigable endeavors, we enjoyed what we convincingly told ourselves was the best linguini and white clam sauce we ever had. Actually, the outing was nothing more than a rationalization on our part because we had to justify all that time and energy spent searching senselessly for a plateful of fresh clams. Since that day, after purchasing a clam rake and checking the local tide, we became a bit more productive. However, we had never really scored *big*. We had never hit the mother lode. Why? The simple answer is because we didn't try hard enough. Oh, we put in a good hour (times two souls) working each side of a low tide, but we didn't take the time to explore new areas that might hold more of those delectable morsels. Instead, we worked places that had been worked over by the populace. What could we really have expected? We didn't have so-called secret spots that produced scores of clams in a matter of an hour like some folks claimed they had. We kept to known places—well and widely known to most everyone.

If you think fishermen keep their secret haunts to themselves, try eliciting a sweet clamming spot from a clam digger. If he happened to inadvertently blab this coveted information to you after several cocktails, he'd probably be contemplating *digging* your grave during his first sobering thought. One dearly departed friend, Bob Johnsen, in addition to an affable acquaintance of ours, had continually refused to reveal their hot, sweet, clamming spot(s) to Donna and me. Not only will I tell you how I finally obtained one coveted area, I'll tell you what it cost me. You won't pay nearly as high a price if you heed some sound advice. Promise.

It was July 15th of 2007. The wind was horrific and whitecaps were building rapidly on the Peconic River in back of our home. I saw that a neighbor's friend's boat (the acquaintance previously mentioned) was in trouble. He was having difficulty docking, and I ran to help him. I grabbed a line and simply looped it over a stern cleat after fighting both the wind and tide. "Neutral," I called out. When the vessel was alongside the dock and relatively secure, I removed the stern loop and was in the process of belaying it properly by placing it under and then back over the cleat to be made fast. Possibly figuring that I needed further assistance in countering the elements, perhaps anxious that his boat would be blown back away from the dock, the captain abruptly engaged the throttle, inadvertently sending the 26-foot cruiser windward in a left-rudder-reverse maneuver. I lost a third of a middle finger on my left hand. There were lessons to be learned from the experience.

My acquaintance, of course, felt terrible, asking repeatedly, week after week, what he could do for me. I told him that there was nothing he could do and to please stop beating up on himself. This went on for a month until I finally said, "All right, I know exactly what you can do for me." He said, "Anything. Just name it." I told him I wanted to know where his clamming spot was; that *secret* location! Without blinking an eye, he said that better than just telling me, he'd take both Donna and me there. And he did. Donna, for the most part, pulled around the floating basket as we handed her clam after clam. Practically every other pull—dig—lift—produced a clam. I was as happy as a clam at high tide, just not as quiet. Occasionally, we picked up two and three clams at a clip. Two of us working two rakes for two hours turned up one hundred thirty clams! Some folks would give an arm and a leg for a secret, sweet clamming spot. I only gave up a third of a finger. Yes, you've got to maintain a sense of humor about such incidents. Another lesson learned (after Donna and I garnered a bit more confidence) was that when the two of us finally got off of our duffs, we found our own secret hot spot. We had promised our acquaintance—now a very good friend—Brendan Byrne, that we would not reveal *his* spot, and we're true to our word. But I did share Donna's and my *new* secret spot with a fellow with whom I used to fish. I take no umbrage in that he calls me Short-Fingered Bob while projecting a gravelly gangster-like voice. I just smile and clam up.

Keeping a log of your outdoor activities, be it fishing, clamming or crabbing [the latter to discussed in the following chapter], will provide you with important information for future outings that if went unrecorded might prove nothing more than a pleasant yet distant memory. By keeping an accurate accounting of your excursions, you will be quite surprised and pleased to see a pattern emerge that will aid in enhancing your abilities and enjoyment. Just short of revealing our *secret* locations, you will see that in most cases Donna and I quickly became more productive as we proceeded. Too, you will note how we truly upped our ante by securing a second clam rake. Not just any clam rake, but one better suited to securing more clams. The initials below, DD and BB, belong to Donna and me; then later, to those of fellow clammers. Where you see two sets of initials but only one rake, it means that one of us is trailing a container while the other digs for clams. Hence, the designated hours are to be interpreted as man-hours per rake, not the number of persons per se.

June 25th, 2008. Fishing was off. Headed to our clamming area(s); 2.5 hours; 1 rake operation 36 clams; all sizes; BB, DD
June 27th, 2008. 3.5 hours; 1 rake–47 clams; BB, DD
June 30th, 2008. 4.5 hours; 1 rake–90 clams; BB
July 3rd, 2008. 4.25 hours; 2 rake operation–133 clams; BB, DD, GF, SF
July 10th, 2008. 2.75 hours; 1 rake–48 clams; BB, DD
July 18th, 2008. 3 hours; 1 rake–51 clams; BB, DD
July 22nd, 2008. 5 hours; 3 rake operation–193 clams; 8 scallops; BB, DD, SF
August 3rd, 2008. 3 hours; 1 rake–50 clams; BB, DD
August 19th, 2008. 3 hours; 3 rakes–101 clams; BB, DD, GF, SF
August 21st, 2008. 3.5 hours; 2 rakes–211 clams; GF, SF

August 22nd, 2008. Donna and I decide to purchase that second rake. We are taken to a *secret* spot by two other *secretive* souls: Bob Johnsen and a female friend. Bob finally broke down and took Donna and me to his secret area. 1 hour; 4 rake operation–<u>339</u> clams. Wow! BB, DD dug up 227 clams; BJ, LW 112 clams. We were sworn to secrecy and may only visit that spot by special invitation.

Note: A good part of our success I attribute to the new rake's comfort and wider design. The new rake outproduced our old rake by a considerable margin. Compare the old So Lo rake to our new Ribb rake. It was purchased for $70.55 (including tax) from White's Hardware Store in Greenport. It paid for itself after a couple of outings.

Back to our old spots:

September 2nd, 2008. 3 hours; 1 rake (new)–73 clams; 1 scallop; BB
September 3rd, 2008. 4.5 hour; 1 rake (new)–97 clams; BB
September 12th, 2008. Secret area by BJ's invitation only. Very windy and rainy. 45 minutes; 3 rakes–105 clams; BB, DD: 58 clams–BJ: 47 clams.

The two containers pictured are drilled-out plastic buckets rimmed with Noodles, those closed-cell foam tubes that kids play with in swimming pools. Also, a pair of water shoes is important for foot protection.

You, too, can and will seek out such productive areas for yourselves. Donna and I love this life. Can you dig it?

Chapter 21

CRABBING

Got the summertime fishing doldrums? For diversion on those listless summer days when the fish fail to cooperate, give crabbing a shot. On the north and south forks of Long Island, the summer of 2007 proved to be a bonanza year for blue claw crabs (blue crabs). The blue claws were everywhere in notable numbers: the Peconic River, Reeves Bay, Flanders Bay, Great Peconic Bay, Little Peconic Bay, their creeks, around docks, piers, et cetera. Wherever there was moving water, there were crabs for the taking. Fresh crabmeat accounts for some of the best sea fare beneath the face of our planet. Many folks would agree that those tasty shellfish rate right up there with lobster. Again, just like clamming, you'll want to check the local regulations for Shellfish Harvest Areas, as you may need a permit or license. Keep in mind that good crabbing seasons follow winter freezes. January and February of 2011 were very cold; my log book shows that the months of July, August and September of 2011 proved to be a good crabbing season for Donna and me. Conversely, 2012 was a mild winter on Long Island, so the season did not prove as productive. However, our cold winter of 2013 should prove a banner year for crabs. Keep in mind that Donna and I are not commercial crabbers. Recreational crabbers will have little trouble bringing home table fare for friends and family be it a mild or cold winter.

There are several methods for crabbing: drop lines, killie rings, pull traps, and box traps. I prefer the latter because they draw the most visitors. A box trap is a mini motel magnet for blue claw crabs. After just one descent of the wire unit into a few feet of water for a period of several hours, I could have hung out a No Vacancy sign. On first inspection, more than a dozen occupants had gathered within the cage. From that two-foot cube, I immediately collected those nice size crustaceans (most of them measuring better than 4½ inches from point-to-point across their carapace), released and cleared the cage of the little guys, added fresh bluefish carcasses into the bottom of the plastic disk-covered bait holder running through the center of the plastic-coated wire coop, then reopened for business anew. I was thinking of adding a Vacancy sign for giggles. In just a few hours, Donna and I had seven additional blue claw crabs to add to the steam pot. There was only one thing left to do. Expand the operation by doling out responsibilities.

I contacted neighbors from around the corner. Without telling them exactly what adventure we were to embark upon, I simply asked if the couple wanted to go into *business* with us.

Crab Motel Being Pulled Up From Dockside

"How much venture capital do I need to put up?" the husband inquired with a skeptical look upon his puss.

"Half. Fifteen bucks," I answered.

Without batting an eye, he smiled, opened his wallet, and handed over a sawbuck and a fin.

"You now own half interest in a crabbing operation," I declared. "We share one trap jointly." I then spoke of Donna's and my immediate success. "I believe that a single trap will keep the four of us in crabmeat," I proclaimed.

The agreement was that he and I would take turns placing and checking the trap in one of the bays mentioned above. Donna and she would share the job of steaming and cleaning the crabs. It was a match made in shellfish heaven.

The area in which I had initially placed the trap was still producing nicely; however, out of curiosity, he and I moved that box trap from one place to another throughout the bays. Wherever we set the trap, we scored nicely. Actually, we could have expanded the business that season by purchasing an additional trap as there were crabs everywhere, but we were only interested in taking what we needed to feed our respective families and dear friends—and feed them well we did.

It was like something out of the movie *Forrest Gump*, starring Tom Hanks and his business partner Private Benjamin Buford 'Bubba' Blue, played by Mykelti Williamson. Instead of the latter reciting the infinite ways of preparing shrimp, the four of us rustled up recipes that would give some of the best chefs in the country

136

pause; truly, for the four of us take great pride in preparing and presenting our fine fare to one another. For example: Long Island crab cakes (nevermind Maryland), sautéed crabmeat in white wine and garlic, crabs with marinara sauce over linguine, crabmeat salad, crab quiches and soufflés, deviled crabs, crabs gumbo, crab stew, crabs ad infinitum. You've heard of U-pick shrimp whereby you shell your own. Well, for a simple but messy outdoors repast, try hammering your way to heaven; that is, malleting your meal—consisting of freshly steamed crabs spread upon a picnic table covered with brown wrapping paper. It's certainly easy cleanup; meaning the table. You, however, may require a shower—unless you have witnessed Gallagher's appearances on television and know how to prepare for such an event. Bibs or aprons are practically mandatory. And when your guests show up and see the table set with mallets in lieu of traditional silverware, well, your afternoon is sure to be filled with fun. But better serve and finish up early before the mosquitoes finish you off first and foremost.

Having a smaller more portable pull trap aboard a boat, or simply carried from the trunk of a vehicle to a dock or pier, can be a fun way to introduce and teach kids how to catch a few crabs for the dinner table. If the current is strong, you will want to weigh the trap down with lead sinkers attached to the bottom of the cage. This can easily be accomplished with plastic cable ties. A couple of 10-ounce sinkers secured caddy-corner should hold bottom nicely. Lines for these traps usually come in 48-foot lengths. A 5-gallon plastic Spackle or detergent bucket is ideal for *temporarily* holding and transporting those crabs home. However, if you plan on being away for several hours, especially in the heat of day, you would be well-advised to do one of two things. Either place the crabs in a cooler layered with ice and newspaper, or submerge a specially prepared 5-gallon bucket to hold and keep your prizes alive until you're ready to leave.

Here is how to fashion that container and lid: With a hole saw, drill out a dozen or so one-inch diameter holes around the sides of the bucket. Out of quality braided 3/8-inch nylon line, construct a hinge for the lid, a loop opposite the hinge in order to lock it to the bucket, and a handle for convenient transporting. Forget about bungee cords and cords per se; they rot and break over a period of time. Better to do things once and do it right—right from the start.

In order to hinge the lid to the container, simply drill one 3/8-inch hole near the rim of the lid. Drill a second 3/8-inch hole near the top edge of the container. Next, run a short section of line through both holes, adjusting its length properly so that you can lift and close the lid evenly. Tie off then burn and melt the ends to keep them from fraying. Opposite the hinge, repeat step one with a section of line necessary to lock the lid securely. Tie off; burn and melt the ends.

Along both sides of the container, drill a 3/8-inch hole. Run a rope line for a handle in lieu of any metal handle, using the same procedure as you did for the hinge. With an additional length of line tied to the rope handle, suspend your crabby prizes in the suds until you are ready to head home. This will keep those crabs fresh and feisty. Then simply transfer the crabs into the first bucket so as not to have a mess.

Aboard our boat, I use an ice chest for storing the crabs and for easy transport. Place ice—cubes work best as you want the crabs kept relatively level—in the bottom of the cooler. A five-pound bag should suffice for a small chest. Keep the drain plug open. Layer the crabs between sheets of newspaper. This way, if you pick up an occasional soft-shell crab, you can isolate and insulate it from the others as they can puncture and kill their recently molted relative when thrashing about. When you're ready to leave, remember to close the drain plug. Your crabs will stay nice and fresh and secure in their storage chest as you travel home.

A pair of long-handled tongs, a steamer pot with a couple inches of water, and a tablespoon or two of crab boil (a spice mixture) is all you need to start the cooking process. Fifteen minutes is the magic number. Just be sure and check that you have enough water in the pot.

The simplest way I know of to start kids *crabbing* (no, I don't mean their incessant, "Are we there yet, Dad?" whining) is to merely tie a chicken leg or neck to a string, lower it to a watery floor from a dock, pier or boat—and wait. Let the young child's mind wonder and wander off to special places like the movie *Finding Nemo*, or God forbid, *Jaws*! Five or ten minutes later, have the child gently lift the line towards the surface, with mom or dad at the ready with a long-handled net should the treasure be hanging there by a thread. Parents new to crabbing need little instruction: Carefully maneuver the net towards and beneath the unsuspecting crab as the galvanized child gently and steadily raises the critter to the surface. God help you if you miss, Mom; shame on you if you delay, Dad. The disappointment will be clearly written on their precious but perturbed faces. Not to worry. Practice does make perfect . . . most times. You'll be exonerated in no time flat. Just lighten up on the kids if in their excitement they pull suddenly instead of lift . . . gingerly.

Later, everyone may want to graduate to a killie ring. This basically employs the same method but requires slipping one end of the ring through the gills of several bantam size baitfish such as killies, spearing, sand eels, peanut bunker, et cetera. The ring is simply a stiff length of wire (such as a coat hanger) that is fashioned into a circle. Bend both ends back so as to form a lock when joined together. Whatever method of crabbing one employs, I believe it's for kids from ages six to eighty-plus. As a matter of fact, many years ago, I went crabbing with my eighty-five-year-old fishing buddy, Emiel. He was the oldest kid I ever knew. May he rest in peace.

It is rather unfortunate that certain folks will not bother with blue claw crabs because it requires some effort when it comes to cleaning them. The word effort translates into work. Initially, that is true. However, with a bit of practice, that task becomes practically effortless if you adopt a certain mind-set. Keep in mind that crabmeat rivals lobster meat. That is a fact. With practice, a newcomer can pick the meat out of twelve nice size crabs in about an hour and a quarter, which will yield approximately a pound of meat. Try and find a market that will even sell you *fresh* crabmeat in our neck of the woods and waters. You won't! I'm not talking about canned or frozen crabmeat. I'm talking about real *fresh* crabmeat.

When those inflexible proprietors of several fish markets were pressed for a dollar amount for the sake of a hypothetical comparison, I was quoted prices ranging between $40 to $60 a pound if they *were* to (again, speaking theoretically) perform the process, which they flatly refused to do. And that's for the cleaning alone. Add to that the cost of each crab at approximately $3.50 apiece. That's an additional $42 a dozen for a grand total of $82 dollars a pound! To say that this cost would be prohibitive is certainly an understatement. To say that it would be a form of waterway robbery if the proprietor would even bother to accommodate his or her customers is closer to the truth. So, the point remains moot.

Once again, with a bit of practice, you could clean those dozen blue claws in an hour and a quarter. If you could *reel* in one additional member of your family to assist you, then we are talking less than three quarters of an hour. Keep in mind that when you order crab cakes or say flounder stuffed with crabmeat in your local restaurant, or even at your local seafood market, for the most part you are getting sea legs; that is, surimi (generally from pollock) in lieu of crabmeat. Many folks know this, yet most of us fall into the trap of ordering spuriously, as if we are truly getting fresh crabmeat in our fare, especially at those moderately priced restaurants. If you head for Maryland or parts of Delaware, things change drastically; the crab cakes down there are the real deal. It's a big industry. They have women who can pick a crab clean in a matter of a minute. The question is whether or not it's worth the extra effort for *you* to enjoy the real McCoy. Donna and I certainly know so.

Food for thought folks—speaking of which, a few of our favorite seafood recipes referencing both shellfish and finfish follow this chapter.

Chapter 22

SEAFOOD RECIPES

Y ou're in for several gourmet treats. I'll begin with this mouth-watering recipe.
Donna and I have always enjoyed clams Casino as well as clams Rockefeller;
therefore, I combined the two to give you . . .

Bobby B's Clams Casino/Rockefeller
(4 full-course servings)

Ingredients:

> 2 dozen freshly shucked and coarsely chopped cherrystone clams
> ½ stick butter
> 2 tablespoons olive oil
> 2 cloves garlic (minced)
> ½ cup finely diced red bell pepper
> ½ cup finely diced green bell pepper
> 1 tablespoon finely chopped shallot
> ½ cup heavy cream
> ½ cup white wine
> 9 oz. fresh or frozen creamed spinach
> ½ cup seasoned bread crumbs
> ¼ cup freshly grated fontina cheese
> ¼ cup freshly grated Swiss Gruyére cheese
> 6 strips thin sliced bacon
> 2 tablespoons additional bread crumbs to finish topping bacon strips
> 3 tablespoons finely chopped parsley

Procedure:

On a baking sheet lined with slightly crumpled heavy-duty aluminum foil, place two
dozen empty clam shell halves. The foil will keep the shells level, preventing any
juices from spilling, and will facilitate easy cleanup.

Atop each clam shell half, place a teaspoon of cooked creamed spinach.

In a large Teflon skillet, add the butter and olive oil; lightly sauté the diced red and green pepper followed by the onion and garlic. Add the heavy cream, white wine, bread crumbs, fontina and Swiss Gruyére cheeses. Cook over low heat until the cheeses melt.

Combine the mixture well and fill each clam shell. Top with one-third strip <u>thinly</u> sliced bacon and sprinkle lightly with bread crumbs.

Place the clams under a high broil and cook until the bacon is crisp and the bread crumbs turn brown to slightly blackened.

Remove from broiler and sprinkle with parsley. Serve immediately. Your guests will flip.

Note: With thicker sliced bacon, you'll have to monitor and turn so as to broil evenly on both sides. No one wants to eat partially cooked bacon.

Serving Suggestion: Serve as a main course (six clams casino/Rockefeller per serving) with pasta, or as an appetizer (three clams per serving), cutting the recipe in half.

Bon Appétit!

Bobby B's Gourmet Manhattan Clam Chowder: 21 + 2 Secret Ingredients
(Serves 8)

Ingredients:

24 shucked, coarsely chopped cherrystone clams and their liquid
2 (28 oz.) cans San Marzano whole peeled plum tomatoes
½ cup red bell pepper finely chopped
½ cup green bell pepper finely chopped
½ cup red onion finely chopped
½ cup celery finely chopped
½ cup frozen super sweet corn kernels
½ cup frozen peas
½ cup frozen cut green beans
½ package frozen leaf spinach
½ cup white potato, diced
½ cup bacon coarsely chopped
½ cup fresh coarsely chopped parsley

7 cloves finely chopped garlic
2 tbsp. oregano
2 tbsp. basil
splash of dry red wine
dash of ground fresh pepper
dash of Old Bay
dash of ground cayenne red pepper (careful)

Now, for the *piéces de résistance*; namely, two (2) additional ingredients, for a shrewd chef always leaves out one or more ingredients when asked his or her secret recipe:

½ cup Prosciutto di Parma coarsely chopped
½ cup porcini mushrooms finely chopped

Procedure:

In an 8-quart pot, lightly mash the whole peeled plum tomatoes.

Combine <u>all</u> of the ingredients and simmer for two hours. If needed, thin contents with low-salt chicken broth. Do not add water or additional clam juice to thin out contents as the soup may become somewhat diluted and/or salty.

Parmesan cheese, grated, to top off soup at the table.

Buon Appetito!

Bobby B's Littleneck Clams in Black Bean Sauce
(Appetizer for 4)

Ingredients:

2 dozen littleneck clams
2 cups drained and washed black beans
½ cup cream sherry
1 tablespoon grated fresh ginger
1 minced clove of garlic
½ small finely chopped jalapeño pepper
¼ teaspoon sesame seed oil
1 teaspoon soy sauce

½ teaspoon raw sugar
1 6.5 oz. jar marinated artichoke hearts (half each precut slice ~ 8 pieces)
2 one-eighth inch thick slices of prosciutto cut into one-by-one inch strips
½ cup half-and-half
2 finely chopped (green section) scallions

Procedure:

Shuck the clams and leave whole in bottom half of shells. Discard top shells.

Marinate the black beans in sherry, ginger, garlic, jalapeño pepper, sesame seed oil, soy sauce and sugar for 45 minutes, then purée.

Place purée and artichoke pieces in a large sauté pan ~ add the clams on the half shell. Cook for 7 minutes over medium/low heat.

Set aside remaining ingredients: prosciutto, half-and-half, scallions. Note that you have three separate colors: red, white and green. This is my special Italian/Oriental creation.

Raise the heat to medium and simmer the purée for approximately another 5 minutes. Bring the pan to the table and, before your guests, carefully fold in those three remaining ingredients, spooning the *entire* contents over the clams. Serve immediately and graciously accept a series of approval and applause.

Bobby B's Crab Cakes
(Serves 4)

Ingredients:

1 pound lump crabmeat
1½ cups panko (Japanese) bread crumbs
2 tablespoons chopped parsley
2 tablespoons chopped scallion
3 eggs
1 tablespoon lemon juice
1 teaspoon dry mustard
1 teaspoon Worcestershire sauce
¼ teaspoon cayenne pepper
½ teaspoon Kosher salt
1/3 cup olive oil

1 cup additional panko bread crumbs

Procedure:

Place crabmeat, 1½ cups panko bread crumbs, parsley and scallion in a bowl. Set aside.

In a separate bowl, whisk together eggs, lemon juice, dry mustard, Worcestershire sauce, cayenne and salt. Combine with crabmeat mixture, carefully using a wooden spoon, being careful not to break up the lump crab meat.

Form cakes and cover entirely with remaining 1 cup panko bread crumbs. Chill for one hour.

Fry crab cakes in olive oil over medium heat for 4 minutes or until golden brown.

Place cakes onto paper towels to drain.

Enjoy!

Donna's Crab Quiche
(Serves 6)

Ingredients:

Pie Crust

1 cup all-purpose flour (King Arthur brand is preferred)
½ teaspoon salt
1/3 cup shortening (unsalted butter)
3-6 tablespoons ice water
9-inch pie pan, preferably Pyrex

Procedure:

Combine the flour and salt with a pastry cutter/blender until mixture resembles coarse crumbs.

Sprinkle the flour mixture with water, one teaspoon at a time, mixing lightly with a fork. Continue adding the ice water until the mixture is moist enough to form into a ball when lightly pressed together.

Shape the dough into a ball; flatten on a floured surface to a ½-inch thickness.

Roll out the dough evenly, working from the center to the edge, approximately 1½ inches wider than the pie pan when inverted. Place gently into pie pan; set aside.

Ingredients:

Filling:
2 cups cheese (use either Swiss, Jarlsberg, white cheddar, or any other cheese you wish); cut into thin strips
2 tablespoons flour
4 eggs
1½ cups half-and-half
¼ cup chopped white onions
6 slices cooked crumbled bacon
8 ounces picked blue claw crabmeat
dash of ground black pepper to taste

Procedure:

Set oven to 350 degrees.

Toss the cheese with flour.

In a separate bowl, slightly beat the eggs with a fork. Add half-and-half, onion, bacon, pepper, crabmeat and cheese. Mix very well.

Pour mixture into pastry-lined pan. Bake for 40-45 minutes or until a knife inserted into its center comes out clean. Let cool about 10 minutes before serving.

*Variation: Add chopped red bell pepper, chopped green bell pepper and diced Virginia ham or prosciutto. Our favorite is prosciutto di Parma.

Bon Appétit!

Bobby B's Baked Striped Bass
(Serves 4 to 6)

Normally, when we flour, egg and breadcrumb fish fillets, we fry them. But here's an alternate method that is truly delicious.

Ingredients:

> 4 striped bass fillets (2 to 3 + pound equivalent)
> 2 eggs
> flour for dredging
> breadcrumbs for dredging; approximately 2 tablespoons additional for sauce
> ¼ cup dry white wine
> 4 pats butter (½-inch wide from a quarter pound stick)
> 3 teaspoons olive oil
> juice from ½ lemon
> 2 cloves garlic, sliced thin
> 1 tablespoon fresh chopped parsley for garnish

Procedure:

Coat fillets with flour, whisked eggs and breadcrumbs. Refrigerate for 30 minutes.

Place fillets in a baking dish covered with non-stick aluminum foil.

Place butter, white wine, lemon juice, garlic and two tablespoons of breadcrumbs in the baking dish, surrounding the fillets. Cover the pats of butter with olive oil.

Bake for approximately 20 minutes (depending on thickness) at 375 degrees. Test for *near*-doneness.

Place under broiler for 2 minutes just to color the breadcrumbs to a golden brown. Fish should be flaky yet moist.

Cover the fillets with sauce spooned from the baking dish. Garnish lightly with parsley.

Serve immediately.

Enjoy!

Bobby B's Broiled Porgy Parmigiana
(Serves 4)

Ingredients:

1¼ pounds of porgy fillets
1 tablespoon of lemon juice
2 tablespoons of virgin olive oil
¼ cup grated Parmesan cheese
2 tablespoons mayonnaise
2 scallions, chopped very fine
1 cup melted butter ~ room temperature
dashes of salt and freshly ground black pepper to taste
2 tablespoons chopped parsley
1 lemon, thinly sliced.

Procedure:

Mix the cheese, mayonnaise, salt, butter and scallions in a small bowl and set aside.

Lightly coat a baking dish with olive oil and place fillets in a single layer; brush fish with lemon juice.

Broil fillets 4 to 6 minutes or until fish flakes easily with a fork.

Remove from oven and spread with cheese mixture.

Broil about 30 seconds longer or until cheese is lightly browned and bubbly.

Garnish with sliced lemon and parsley and serve immediately.

This simple but delicious recipe may be used for virtually any filleted fish you choose. Very tasty!

Bon Appétit!

Chapter 23

SMOKING FISH

Char-Broil Charcoal Water-Marinade Smoker Method

As we near the end of this book, it would be fitting to conclude with a marvelous method for preparing your favorite fish. The technique of smoking ranks supreme. Fresh fish lend themselves to the art of smoking and are true delicacies. In this final chapter, we'll cover the equipment and materials plus everything you need to know to get started.

Smoking Fresh Fish Fillets

Generally speaking, shortcuts shortchange the multitude, be it a meal or a methodology. However, once in a blue moon, a more expeditious technique of handling something otherwise tedious and time consuming comes along that may surprise us. Charcoal water smokers are one such example. In this day and age, where time is not to be squandered, mediocrity often takes the place of perfection. I have been smoking fish for a good many years. Therefore, the methods, means and recipes employed throughout that period of time are not just occurrences that were repeated a few times successfully; rather, they have evolved over several decades. Each facet has been time-tested, fine-tuned, tweaked then given the seal of approval by discerning folks who grace our table regularly. Those friends, familiars, and acquaintances share one thing in common. They are no-nonsense, straightforward souls, meaning that they are a breed who say what they mean and mean what they say. For example: "Bob, this fish fillet and sauce are really fantastic."—or—"Bob, nail it to a board, smoke it some more, then throw away the fish and eat the board!" I wouldn't have it any other way; that is, the advice—not the board.

During mid-spring and early fall runs of bluefish, blackfish, sea bass, fluke, flounder, mackerel, weakfish, stripers and eels in our local waters, I get the craving for fresh smoked fish. Not that the summer season sells us short; it is just too darn hot to be fussing around with firewood and coals. But when the cooler weather arrives, there is nothing quite like the smell, texture and taste of smoked fresh fish. As a rule of thumb, oily fish such as bluefish, mackerel and salmon smoke particularly well. However, do not overlook the more delicate flesh and flavor of fluke, flounder and striped bass; otherwise, you will be missing out on a rare treat.

One evening, my soul mate and I had nailed some big-shouldered linesiders in the twenty-five to thirty pound range. Several of those steaks and fine fillets were planned for the table; others found their way to our smoker. In the past, we had smoked a ton of saltwater species, including our fair share of freshwater trout, largemouth and smallmouth bass. All are quite excellent fare. The magic? TLC; that is, Tender Loving Care. It begins from the moment you pick your prizes from the waters. Bleeding your catch, especially bluefish, is of paramount importance whether it is for the smoker, barbecue grill or the frying pan. Iced down or placed in a cooler with cube or block ice will ensure freshness until you return home—especially during those hot summer days.

Over the years, I have experimented with various brines in which to marinate poultry and red meat. Brining fish is a somewhat different story, for you want to enhance its flavor, not mask it. Herbs and spices and even your choice of wood for smoking fish can hinder its fine taste. Bluefish, contrary to what some folks believe, do not warrant disguising in any way, shape or form when preparing them for the smoker. Keeping your ingredients simple and materials basic is the way to proceed. However, I would like to introduce you to a tool that is worth its weight in mako meat, to be used on fish, fowl or red meat in order to cut both the marinating and cooking/smoking time by forty to fifty percent—for real! It's called the Jaccard and sold primarily as a meat tenderizing machine, although it boasts, too, tenderizing the flesh of fish. I wouldn't be caught preparing fare without this tool. For example, whereas whole cocktail-size blues or fish fillets ordinarily require approximately six hours of brining time (twelve hours for very thick fillets or large whole fish), you can cut that curing time in half by first using the Jaccard.

Also, you can limit the time attending to the smoker unit by selecting and soaking large chunks of wood or woodchips in lieu of splinters of wood. For decades, I had smoked virtually all my fish in an improvised barbecue grill/water pan setup. Years later, I chiefly smoked whole fish with my Little Chief home electric smoker. Occasionally, I still do. However, the process was initially long and tedious until I devised a way to expedite the cooking/smoking process without sacrificing quality. I'll cover that technique momentarily, as the electric unit does have a distinct advantage.

These days, for smoking fresh fish fillets I use a Char-Broil model 06701289 Charcoal Water-Marinade Smoker. I now smoke three times the amount of fish, fowl and/or game in a fraction of the time, which is certainly a godsend. Believe me when I tell you that I would not sacrifice perfection for any amount of time saved. It is simply not worth it to me, nor should it be to you. I offer kudos to this marvelous cylindrical unit that measures approximately 17 inches in diameter and stands 30 inches high. At approximately $40 at Home Depot, this unit is definitely a bargain.

The charcoal/wood, water-marinade unit may be used in three ways: as a grill (cooking directly over the fire in the high-heat range), as a barbecue (cooking in the medium range), or as a smoker (cooking at a temperature in the low range). Additionally, the unit has two cooking grates, which allow you to really stack up your favorite fare for a feast fit for a king and queen. Your minions will love you and may

Char-Broil Charcoal Water-Marinade Smoker

not even ask for cake as they will be replete with fine food done to a turn. Essentially, all you do is prepare the brine solution, start the coals or briquettes in the bottom pan, collect your favorite wood chunks, add a seasoned water-marinade to the pan above it, and act kingly.

One fine morning, Donna and I caught four nice cocktail blues on spinning and fly rod outfits. I filleted the fish (scaled but not skinned), prepared a brine solution, and readied the smoker. The Char-Broil Charcoal Water-Smoker allows you to hot-smoke your food efficiently, whereas before I had to allow a minimum of half to a full day to effectively accomplish what I can now do in a few hours.

Once again, that handy little tool I mentioned a moment ago will save you several hours when brining and smoking fish, fowl and red meat. The Jaccard is available in two models: a mini Jaccard with one row of sixteen blades, and the larger model with three rows containing forty-eight blades. No contest in deciding which tool to order. We elected to purchase the larger model and are certainly glad we did. If cost is a factor, well, then that's another story.

Before we actually begin the brining and cooking process, understanding the chemistry of smoking fish will make you more proficient as there are several variables to consider. Without getting too technical, brining draws out the moisture from the product, consequently changing its texture and making the flesh denser. Oily fish such as bluefish, mackerel, salmon, et cetera are not as dry as non-fatty fish after brining and smoking. All things being equal, striped bass, weakfish, fluke, flounder and freshwater trout, for example, require less time in the smoker.

What happens chemically in the smoking process is a reaction between formaldehyde from the burning wood and the protein found in the flesh of the fish. The result is a firm texture, initially generated by the brining process in order to create a thin, filmy, sticky glaze or gelatin—termed a pellicle, from Latin, meaning skin. Additionally, keeping the fish's skin on the fillet prevents the flesh from drying out; also, it helps hold the strip together.

Scaling your fish, unless we're talking eels or catfish and such, will prevent a mess. Common sense you say? I guess I wasn't gifted in that department because as a young fellow I either forgot or simply didn't know. The second time out, I removed the skin from the fillets but quickly learned that leaving it on is a far better way to proceed for the reasons stated above. Place the skin-side <u>down</u> upon the grate; do not turn the fillets. I'm sure I don't have to mention that the cooking/smoking process is done outdoors.

There are basically two methods of smoking foods: hot and cold/cool. Hot-smoking is a process that sufficiently flavors and cooks fish, red meat and poultry. One procedure, the one with which we will concern ourselves, requires a smoking temperature of around 180 to 200 degrees Fahrenheit for at least thirty minutes, but we must certainly smoke our product considerably longer in order to flavor and dry—not dry out—our fare.

Another method flavors the product but does not actually cook it, calling for a temperature of approximately 140 degrees. An additional procedure is one that lightly scents the food but then relies on another type of cooking in order to finish it off. Cold-cooking, sometimes referred to as cool-cooking, calls for the food to be frozen first in order to rid it of parasites. It is then smoked at a temperature below 90 degrees. The latter piping process usually necessitates the transference of smoke from a hot smoker into that of a second receptacle containing the items in order to retain that low temperature. I briefly mention the whole ball of wax concerning these methods of operation in order for you to have a basic understanding of smoking foods and to avoid any confusion, confusion with regard to which method offers the best product. In my opinion and the opinions of many other folks (for one must have guinea pigs in order to establish what is good and what is fair to middling), the 180 to 200 degree method of hot-smoking gets my vote and wins hands down!

The convenient temperature gauge atop the Char-Broil smoker's dome takes the guesswork out of the process. Also, an easy-access 8 x 5-inch door leading to the fuel and water pans facilitates the ease of operation. For evenness, you can control the cooking/smoking process by adding more coals and wet wood chunks. Too, you can adjust the top vent in the dome or open the door for more air so as to control the burn rate. Allowing the water in the pan to evaporate will increase the temperature for the final drying step, which I will discuss shortly.

Below are the items and ingredients you will need, less the Jaccard, which is, of course, optional. No rocket science here, folks. Patience and TLC are the key ingredients. Just give yourself the time needed as will be described here in detail.

We'll start with fish fillets. Over the years, trial and error have resulted in a more than satisfying product, which you can duplicate, producing gourmet quality fare that you will be proud to serve to your family and guests.

Ingredients, Equipment & Materials:

1. First off, you will need, of course, some fresh fish fillets, scaled and the skin left intact.

2. Next, a 2-quart saucepan with a brine solution comprised of ¾ cup kosher salt, one cup dark brown sugar, 3 cups cold water.

3. A tray of ice cubes.

4. A flat, shallow, nonreactive dish such as stainless steel, porcelain or glass—large enough to contain the fillets—will serve nicely. Avoid using metal, as its properties can react with the brine solution.

5. The Char-Broil Charcoal Water-Smoker or comparable hot-smoker unit. Your owner's manual should offer several suggestions, hints and judgment calls.

6. A metal watering can with at least a 6-inch long, narrow pouring spout.

7. Long-handled spatula.

8. A water-filled bucket of wet wood chunks.

Note I: The best woods that I have found for smoking fish are cherry, alder and apple. Mesquite, maple and hickory can overpower the fillets if not used carefully. I personally avoid mixing different woods, selecting one kind.

Note II: I smoked those bluefish fillets to perfection during the first week of August in three-and-a-half hours. You would need to allow yourself a bit more cooking/smoking time in late October when the mercury drops, and experimenting with ambient temperature and time.

9. I prefer briquettes over regular charcoal: follow directions on bag.

10. An aluminum foil-lined tray placed beneath the smoker will protect the surface on which you are working.

11. Heavy-duty aluminum foil and a nonstick cooking spray, such as Pam, will facilitate cleanup of pans, cooking grates and the unit's interior surface. Line the inside of the pans, not the grates, with the foil.

12. Oven mitts.

13. Long-handled metal tongs to add the coals as necessary.

Procedure:

1. Simmer the brine solution for approximately 5 minutes or until the salt and sugar are completely dissolved; cool for 15 minutes. Add the tray of ice cubes to facilitate the cooling process. Place the fillets, skin-side <u>up</u> in the nonreactive container and pour the entire mixture over the flesh. Refrigerate for three hours if you Jaccarded—six hours if you did not. Simple instructions will accompany the tool.

2. Drain, wash and pat each fillet with a paper towel. Allow to air-dry, <u>flesh side up</u>, for approximately one hour. Use this time to line the pans with foil and to spray the entire inside of the unit with a nonstick cooking spray. Too, spray both sides of the gratings. Again, these three steps will save you considerable cleanup. Drain the water from the bucket of wood chunks. Ignite the coals following the instructions on the bag (charcoal or briquettes). When the coals are ready, place the fillets, <u>skin-side down</u>, upon the grates.

3. Add water from the metal watering can to the marinade pan (the pan above the coals. Add coals and wood as needed.

Note: At some future date, you may wish to experiment with a water/marinade solution.

4. After two to three hours of smoking the fillets between 180 to 200 degrees Fahrenheit, test for texture and flavor. You be the judge. If the fillets are too moist, you will want to heat-dry those pieces until they are done to a turn, meaning that you will take it to a point where you are satisfied with their firmness. Again, consult your owner's manual because different smokers require different procedures. The period of time will be determined by the thickness of the fillets and the ambient temperature.

Note: Next time out, you may want to experiment with different spices, lightly sprinkling the fillets before smoking, and/or creating your own water/marinade mixture as mentioned a moment ago.

A buddy of mine, Tom Wernikowski, came by with a "new and improved" secret batch of spices (which took him years to perfect, too.) Delicious!
"What are the ingredients?" I asked.
"Well, as I told you before, Bob, I'd tell you," he said mischievously, "but then I'd have to kill you!"

Another reason why I prefer the hot-smoked method over others is that this smoked product will keep for at least two weeks or better in the refrigerator if wrapped well and sealed in an airtight container. Vacuum sealing the product and placing it in a zero Fahrenheit freezer will keep it long after our glaciers melt from global warming. If you do not have a vacuum sealer in your home, I order you to order one immediately if not sooner. Check out Cabela's Outfitters, www.cabelas.com

Smoked fishes are indeed versatile, to be enjoyed during breakfast, lunch or dinner. They are absolutely delectable tidbits when placed upon crackers with perhaps thin slices of cheese and offered as hors d'oeuvres. For a simple sauce, whip up four tablespoons of sour cream, two tablespoons of mayonnaise, a dash of fresh horseradish to one's taste, and a spot of ketchup for a bit of color.

Smoking Whole Fish: Little Chief Electric Smoker

For smoking whole fish, my Little Chief home electric smoker is the ticket. Earlier, I stated that the process had been long and tedious. That was because one had to tend to the chip pan every hour for a period, on average, of eight hours and sometimes as long as twelve hours. Eventually, I figured a way to expedite matters, thereby cutting the time in half. Fish-wise, the Little Chief unit allows you to hot-smoke either fillets or whole fish. You may either place small fish or fillets flat upon three 12- x 12-inch racks or remove them to hang large, whole fish by utilizing s-shaped hooks that come with the unit. The best technique is to solidly secure the s-hook in the side of the fish's jawbone, not beneath its chin. Otherwise, the connective cartilage and tissue will deliquesce, and the fish will fall, making quite a mess.

Jaccard and brine whole fish for the smoker no differently than you would for those fillets, except that you will rub a thin layer of kosher salt into the gutted cavity of each fish before beginning the smoking process. Again, that handy little tool I keep mentioning will save you several hours when brining and smoking. As I knew that I had enough time to properly prepare a half-dozen cocktail blues, I elected to seize the day and complete the entire process by evening, whereas with a late start, I would be tending the chip pan into the wee hours.

Selecting and soaking woodchips in lieu of splinters of wood supplied with the unit will dramatically cut your smoking time. Conversely, you do not want to use large wood chunks as with the Char-Broil Charcoal Water-Marinade Smoker. Woodchips of approximately one inch x ½ inch are perfect for the Little Chief smoking unit. Until I started using soaked chips, I had been unnecessarily playing around with dry splinters while minding the pan hourly for a minimum of eight hours. Now, a panful lasts approximately two hours. A second go-around, totaling four hours, normally completes the process, which is certainly a significant difference. Check for doneness after three hours. A rich, golden-brown color should be achieved.

Well, there you have it, folks. I trust that you have received invaluable information in this concise yet comprehensive guide and that it will continue to serve you well over the course of years. Perhaps we'll cross paths while enjoying our cherished pursuits.

NOTES

www.ingramcontent.com/pod-product-compliance
Lightning Source LLC
LaVergne TN
LVHW061223060426
835509LV00012B/1404